SETTING YOUTUBE CHANNEL FOR MY BRAND

EVERYTHING YOU NEED TO KNOW TO GET STARTED ON YOUR YOUTUBE JOURNEY IN 2025

THOMAS JAMES ELLIOTT

First Edition 2025

ISBN 9798309377596

Published by The Curious Film Company

CONTENTS

INTRODUCTION

In an era where digital presence is not just an advantage but a necessity, YouTube stands as a formidable platform for brands to connect with a global audience. As we step into 2025, establishing a YouTube channel for your brand is more crucial than ever. This book serves as a comprehensive guide for individuals and businesses eager to make their mark in the vast universe of online video content. Whether you're a seasoned marketer or a novice entrepreneur, understanding the intricacies of setting up a successful YouTube channel is pivotal.

The landscape of digital media is continually evolving, and with it, the strategies to engage viewers and build a loyal community. This guide delves into the essential components of launching and maintaining a YouTube channel that not only reflects your brand's ethos but also captivates your target audience. From defining your brand's voice and visual identity to optimizing your videos for search engines, every chapter is crafted to equip you with the knowledge and tools needed to thrive.

You'll discover how to create compelling content that resonates with viewers, the importance of consistency, and the role of analytics in shaping your content strategy. Additionally, this book addresses the technical aspects of YouTube, such as video production, editing, and platform navigation, ensuring that you are well-prepared to tackle any challenges that arise.

As you navigate through the pages, you'll gain insights from industry experts and learn from case studies that highlight successful YouTube strategies. This journey is not just about gaining subscribers but about building a community that trusts and values your brand. With dedication and the right approach, your YouTube channel can become a powerful extension of your brand's story, reaching audiences far and wide. Prepare to dive into the dynamic world of YouTube and unlock the potential of video content to elevate your brand to new heights.

Chapter 1: Understanding the YouTube Landscape

THE RISE OF YOUTUBE

Imagine a platform that engages more than two billion users monthly, a place where creativity meets commerce, and where brands can transform their narratives into compelling visual stories. YouTube, since its inception in 2005, has evolved from a simple video-sharing site to a colossal force in the digital marketing world. For businesses and entrepreneurs, this platform presents an unprecedented opportunity to connect with audiences on a global scale, making it an indispensable tool for brand development and customer engagement.

The allure of YouTube lies in its accessibility and reach. Unlike traditional media, which often requires significant investment and resources, YouTube offers a cost-effective avenue for brand exposure. The platform empowers brands, regardless of size, to showcase their products and services directly to their target audience. The democratization of content creation means that anyone with a smartphone and an internet connection can potentially reach millions of viewers, leveling the playing field between small startups and established corporations.

Moreover, YouTube's algorithm is designed to promote content that resonates with viewers, offering brands the chance to go viral and gain traction quickly. This potential for rapid growth is unparalleled in the digital landscape. Videos that capture the audience's attention can lead to increased visibility, driving traffic not only to the channel itself but also to the brand's website and social media platforms. The integration of YouTube with Google's advertising ecosystem further amplifies its effectiveness, allowing brands to target specific demographics with precision and efficiency.

The platform's versatility is another compelling reason for brands to invest in their YouTube presence. Whether through tutorials, testimonials, behind-the-scenes looks, or live streams, YouTube enables brands to convey their message in diverse and engaging formats. This flexibility allows brands to build a more personal connection with their audience, fostering trust and loyalty. As consumers increasingly seek authenticity and transparency from the brands they support, YouTube offers a unique medium to showcase these qualities.

Furthermore, the rise of influencer marketing on YouTube presents another layer of opportunity for brands. Collaborating with content creators who align with the brand's values and target audience can significantly enhance credibility and reach. Influencers have cultivated loyal followings, and their endorsement can sway consumer perceptions and purchasing decisions favorably.

In today's digital age, having a presence on YouTube is not just advantageous; it's essential. The platform's impact on consumer behavior and its ability to drive brand awareness and sales cannot be overstated. As more businesses recognize the potential of YouTube, the competition for attention intensifies. Therefore, setting up a YouTube channel for your brand is not merely an option but a strategic imperative to stay relevant and competitive in the market.

Harnessing the power of YouTube can propel your brand to new heights, transforming how you connect with your audience and ultimately driving growth and success. As you consider the next steps for your brand's digital strategy, embracing the opportunities presented by YouTube could be the key to unlocking your brand's full potential.

WHY YOUTUBE FOR YOUR BRAND

Imagine reaching a global audience with just a click, a platform where your brand's voice can resonate with millions. YouTube, the world's second-largest search engine, offers an unparalleled opportunity for brands to connect, engage, and grow. With over 2 billion logged-in monthly users, YouTube's vast audience is a goldmine for businesses eager to expand their reach and influence. It's not just about numbers; it's about the potential to build a community around your brand.

Why choose YouTube? The platform's dynamic nature allows brands to showcase their personalities, values, and stories through engaging visual content. Unlike traditional media, YouTube provides a space for creativity and authenticity, giving brands the freedom to experiment with different content styles—from educational tutorials and behind-the-scenes glimpses to product reviews and live streams. This flexibility helps you craft a unique brand narrative that resonates with your target audience.

Moreover, YouTube's algorithm is designed to promote content that keeps viewers engaged. By creating high-quality videos that captivate your audience, your brand can benefit from increased visibility and discoverability. YouTube's recommendation system can propel your content to new viewers, amplifying your reach far beyond your existing audience.

Another compelling reason to leverage YouTube is its ability to drive traffic and conversions. Videos are a powerful tool for guiding potential customers through the sales funnel. A well-crafted video can educate viewers about your products or services, demonstrate their value, and ultimately persuade them to make a purchase. YouTube videos can also be seamlessly integrated into your overall digital marketing strategy, complementing your website, social media channels, and email campaigns.

Community engagement is another critical aspect of YouTube that brands can harness. The platform enables direct interaction with your audience through comments, likes, and shares, fostering a sense of community and loyalty among your viewers. By actively engaging with your audience, responding to their feedback, and encouraging discussions, you can build a loyal following that advocates for your brand.

YouTube also provides valuable analytics and insights, allowing you to track your video's performance and understand your audience better. These insights can inform your content strategy, helping you optimize future videos for maximum impact. Understanding who your viewers are, what they enjoy, and how they interact with your content is crucial for refining your approach and achieving your brand goals.

Furthermore, the monetization options available on YouTube can create additional revenue streams for your brand. Through ads, sponsorships, and merchandise sales, you can turn your channel into a profitable venture. This financial incentive adds another layer of motivation to invest time and resources into developing your YouTube presence.

In a digital age where video content reigns supreme, establishing a presence on YouTube is not just an option—it's a necessity. By harnessing the power of YouTube, your brand can tap into a vibrant community, tell compelling stories, and drive measurable results. The potential for growth and success on YouTube is immense, making it an essential platform for any brand looking to thrive in today's competitive landscape.

ANALYZING COMPETITORS

Understanding the landscape of your competition is paramount when setting up a YouTube channel for your brand. It's not just about observing what others are doing; it's about strategically analyzing their strengths, weaknesses, opportunities, and threats to carve out your unique space in the digital realm. In the bustling world of YouTube, where countless brands vie for attention, knowing your competitors inside out can provide you with invaluable insights and a significant edge.

Begin by identifying who your competitors are. These are not just brands that operate in the same industry as you but also those that target the same audience. Use YouTube's search function as a starting point, typing in keywords related to your niche. Notice which channels consistently appear at the top. These are your primary competitors. Additionally, tools like Social Blade can offer a deeper dive into their metrics, such as subscriber count and video views, providing a clearer picture of their reach and influence.

Once you have a list of competitors, delve into their content strategy. Observe the types of videos they produce. Are they focusing on tutorials, vlogs, product reviews, or perhaps interviews? Pay attention to the format and style of these videos. Are they polished and professional, or do they have a more casual, authentic feel? Understanding the content type and style that resonates with their audience can inform your strategy. However, the goal is not to mimic but to differentiate. Look for gaps in their content that you can fill or ways to improve upon their offerings.

Engagement metrics are another critical area to analyze. Look at the number of likes, comments, and shares their videos receive. High engagement can indicate that their content is striking a chord with viewers. Scrutinize the comments section to glean insights into what the audience is saying. Are there recurring compliments or criticisms? This feedback can be a treasure trove of information, revealing what works and what doesn't, and guiding your content creation process.

Furthermore, assess their branding and positioning. How do they present their brand visually and verbally? What is their unique selling proposition? A strong, consistent brand presence can significantly enhance viewer loyalty. Consider how you can craft a branding strategy that not only stands out but also aligns with your brand's values and mission.

Also, evaluate their promotional strategies. How do they leverage social media, collaborations, or SEO to enhance their visibility? Understanding their promotional tactics can inspire your marketing strategies, helping you reach a broader audience and increase your channel's discoverability.

By systematically analyzing your competitors, you can gather critical insights that inform your content strategy, branding, and promotional tactics. This analysis empowers you to create a YouTube channel that not only competes but thrives, offering something fresh and valuable to your audience. Remember, the objective is to learn from your competitors, not to imitate them, ensuring that your brand's unique voice and vision shine through in every piece of content you create.

IDENTIFYING YOUR NICHE

When establishing a YouTube channel for your brand, one of the most critical steps is pinpointing your niche. This decision will set the foundation for your content strategy, audience engagement, and overall success. A well-defined niche not only helps to differentiate your brand in the crowded digital landscape but also attracts a dedicated audience that resonates with your message.

Firstly, consider your brand's core values and expertise. What do you stand for, and what unique perspective can you offer? Your niche should align with your brand's identity and goals, ensuring that your content remains authentic and credible. For instance, if your brand specializes in eco-friendly products, your channel could focus on sustainable living tips, green product reviews, or environmental education.

Next, analyze the competition. Conduct thorough research on existing YouTube channels in your potential niche. Identify what works for them and what gaps you can fill. This step is crucial for understanding the landscape and finding opportunities to offer something distinct. Perhaps there's a lack of comprehensive tutorials, or maybe you can add value by providing expert interviews. By identifying these gaps, you can carve out a space that is uniquely yours.

Audience analysis is equally important. Who are you trying to reach, and what are their interests and pain points? Use tools like YouTube Analytics, Google Trends, and social media insights to gather data on your target audience. Understanding their demographics, preferences, and online behavior will guide you in creating content that not only captures their attention but also keeps them coming back for more.

Moreover, consider the scalability of your niche. While niche markets can be profitable due to their specificity, it's vital to ensure there's enough room for growth. A niche that's too narrow might limit your audience, whereas one that's too broad can dilute your brand's message. Strive for a balance where your niche is specific enough to stand out but broad enough to sustain long-term growth.

Additionally, passion plays a significant role. Choose a niche that excites you and aligns with your interests. Your enthusiasm will translate into your content, making it more engaging and relatable. A passionate creator can inspire and connect with their audience on a deeper level, fostering a loyal community around their brand.

Finally, test and refine your niche over time. As you create content and interact with your audience, you'll gain insights into what resonates and what doesn't. Be open to feedback and willing to adapt your niche as needed. This flexibility can lead to new opportunities and help you stay relevant in a dynamic digital environment.

By carefully identifying your niche, you lay the groundwork for a successful YouTube channel that not only promotes your brand but also builds a community of engaged viewers. This strategic focus will guide your content creation, marketing efforts, and ultimately, your brand's growth on the platform.

Chapter 2: Creating a YouTube Strategy

SETTING CLEAR OBJECTIVES

Launching a YouTube channel for your brand is not merely about uploading videos and hoping for the best. It is a strategic endeavor that requires meticulous planning and execution, grounded in the establishment of clear objectives. Setting concrete goals is the cornerstone of any successful YouTube channel. It provides direction, aligns efforts, and measures success. Without specific objectives, your channel risks becoming directionless, making it difficult to gauge progress or justify the investment of time and resources.

The first step in setting clear objectives is understanding why your brand needs a YouTube channel. Are you looking to increase brand awareness, engage with your audience, educate potential customers, or drive sales? Each of these goals requires a different approach and type of content. For instance, if your primary aim is to increase brand awareness, your content might focus on storytelling and brand values. Conversely, if driving sales is your objective, product demonstrations and testimonials could be more effective.

Once you determine the overarching purpose, break it down into specific, measurable objectives. These should be SMART: Specific, Measurable, Achievable, Relevant, and Time-bound. Instead of a vague goal like 'grow the channel,' aim for something specific, such as 'increase subscriber count by 20% in six months.' This clarity not only helps in crafting content strategies but also in tracking progress and making necessary adjustments.

It is equally important to consider your target audience. Understanding who they are, what they value, and how they consume content will shape your objectives. Conducting audience research through surveys, social media analytics, and competitor analysis can provide valuable insights. Tailor your objectives to align with the interests and behaviors of your target audience, ensuring your channel resonates with them and meets their needs.

Moreover, setting clear objectives allows for better resource allocation. Knowing what you aim to achieve helps in deciding how much time, money, and personnel to dedicate to your YouTube efforts. It enables you to prioritize tasks, ensuring the most critical aspects of your strategy receive the attention they deserve. This strategic allocation of resources maximizes efficiency and effectiveness, ultimately leading to a more successful channel.

Regularly reviewing and adjusting your objectives is also crucial. The digital landscape is ever-evolving, and your brand must adapt to changes in consumer behavior, platform algorithms, and industry trends. Periodic assessments of your objectives ensure they remain relevant and aligned with both your brand's goals and the external environment. This adaptability is key to sustaining long-term success on YouTube.

In essence, setting clear objectives is not just a preliminary step but a continuous process that underpins the success of your YouTube channel. It transforms a simple video-sharing platform into a powerful tool for brand growth and engagement. By defining precise goals, understanding your audience, allocating resources wisely, and remaining adaptable, your brand can harness the full potential of YouTube, achieving impactful and measurable results.

DEFINING YOUR TARGET AUDIENCE

To truly harness the power of YouTube for your brand, understanding your target audience is not just beneficial—it's essential. This step forms the foundation upon which all your content strategy, production, and marketing efforts will be built. Without a clear understanding of who you're speaking to, your message may fall on deaf ears, leading to wasted resources and missed opportunities.

Imagine crafting a video that resonates so deeply with viewers that they not only subscribe to your channel but also become loyal advocates for your brand. This level of engagement starts with knowing exactly who your audience is. Begin by considering the demographics of your ideal viewer. Are they young adults who are tech-savvy, or are they professionals seeking industry insights? Knowing their age, gender, location, and occupation can significantly influence the tone, style, and content of your videos.

Beyond demographics, delve into psychographics—what drives your audience? What are their interests, values, and pain points? Understanding these elements allows you to create content that not only attracts viewers but also keeps them coming back for more. For instance, if your brand is in the health and wellness sector, your audience might be interested in topics like fitness routines, nutritional advice, or mental health tips. Tailoring your content to these interests will not only engage your audience but also establish your brand as a trusted authority in your field.

Another crucial aspect is understanding where your audience spends their time online. Are they active on social media platforms like Instagram or TikTok? Do they participate in online forums or communities related to your niche? Identifying these digital hangouts can provide valuable insights into the type of content that will appeal to them and the best strategies to reach them. It also opens up opportunities for cross-promotion and collaboration with influencers who already have the trust of your target audience.

Consider also the challenges and pain points your audience faces. What problems are they trying to solve, and how can your brand help them? By addressing these challenges directly in your videos, you position your brand as a solution provider, which can significantly enhance viewer engagement and loyalty. This approach not only attracts viewers but also converts them into customers who see your brand as a valuable resource.

Finally, don't underestimate the power of feedback. Engage with your audience through comments, polls, and surveys to gather insights directly from them. This interaction not only provides valuable data but also fosters a sense of community and loyalty. By actively listening to your audience, you can refine your content strategy to better meet their needs and preferences.

In essence, defining your target audience is about creating a detailed profile of your ideal viewer. This profile will guide every decision you make on your YouTube channel, from content creation to marketing strategies. With a clear understanding of who you are speaking to, you can craft messages that resonate, engage, and ultimately drive the success of your brand on YouTube.

CONTENT PLANNING AND SCHEDULING

Imagine your YouTube channel as a vibrant city bustling with activity, where each video serves as a building block contributing to the skyline of your brand's presence. To construct this city, a well-thought-out content plan is your blueprint, and scheduling acts as the project timeline ensuring everything comes together seamlessly. Crafting a strategic content plan is not just about filling your channel with videos; it's about creating a cohesive narrative that resonates with your audience and aligns with your brand's objectives.

Begin by identifying the core themes that align with your brand's mission and values. These themes should be broad enough to allow for creativity but focused enough to maintain consistency. For instance, if your brand revolves around sustainable living, your themes might include eco-friendly product reviews, DIY sustainability projects, and interviews with environmental activists. By establishing clear themes, you create a framework that guides content creation and ensures your videos consistently reflect your brand's ethos.

Once themes are established, delve into the specifics of content planning. This involves brainstorming video ideas, researching trending topics within your niche, and analyzing competitor content to identify gaps you can fill. Create a content calendar that outlines when each video will be published, ensuring a steady stream of content that keeps your audience engaged. This calendar should be a living document, flexible enough to accommodate timely content related to current events or trending topics that could boost your channel's visibility.

Scheduling is the backbone of your content plan, turning your creative ideas into a reliable publishing routine. Consistency is key in building an audience on YouTube; viewers are more likely to subscribe and stay engaged if they know when to expect new content. Determine the frequency of your uploads based on your capacity to produce high-quality videos and your audience's consumption habits. Whether it's weekly, bi-weekly, or monthly, stick to a schedule that is sustainable for your team and appealing to your audience.

Utilize scheduling tools available on platforms like YouTube Studio to automate your uploads, ensuring they go live at optimal times when your audience is most active. Analyze your channel's analytics to determine these peak times, which can vary based on your target demographic. Scheduling tools not only help maintain consistency but also free up time for you to focus on content creation and strategy.

Furthermore, engage your audience by teasing upcoming videos through social media or community posts on your channel. This not only piques interest but fosters a sense of anticipation and connection with your viewers. Encourage feedback and suggestions for future content, making your audience feel valued and involved in your channel's growth.

In essence, content planning and scheduling are not mere administrative tasks but pivotal strategies that shape the success of your YouTube channel. They provide direction, consistency, and the ability to adapt, forming the foundation upon which your brand can build a thriving online community. By meticulously planning your content and adhering to a strategic schedule, you lay the groundwork for a channel that not only attracts viewers but transforms them into loyal advocates for your brand.

ALIGNING WITH BRAND GOALS

Crafting a successful YouTube channel for your brand is not just about creating content; it's about ensuring that every piece of content aligns seamlessly with your brand's overarching goals. Every video, every description, and every interaction on your channel should serve a purpose that ties back to the fundamental objectives of your brand. This alignment is crucial in establishing a coherent and recognizable brand presence that resonates with your target audience.

Understanding your brand's goals is the first step in this alignment process. Are you looking to increase brand awareness, drive traffic to your website, boost sales, or perhaps educate your audience about a particular topic? Clearly defining these goals will inform the kind of content you produce and how you present it. For instance, if your primary aim is to educate, your videos should be informative, well-researched, and presented in a way that is accessible and engaging to your audience.

Once your goals are clear, the next step is to ensure that your channel's aesthetic and messaging are consistent with your brand identity. This includes everything from your channel art and logo to the language and tone used in your videos and descriptions. Consistency in these elements helps in building a strong brand image that viewers can easily recognize and relate to. It's about creating a visual and narrative style that reflects your brand's values and personality.

Moreover, aligning with brand goals involves being strategic about the types of content you produce. Consider creating a content calendar that outlines the topics and formats that best align with your objectives. For example, if your goal is to position your brand as a thought leader in your industry, you might focus on creating in-depth analysis videos or interviews with industry experts. On the other hand, if the goal is to increase engagement and build a community, interactive content such as Q&A sessions or live streams might be more effective.

Another critical aspect of alignment is understanding your target audience. Knowing who they are, what they value, and how they interact with content online can help tailor your videos to meet their expectations and needs. This not only helps in retaining viewers but also in converting them into loyal customers or advocates for your brand. Audience insights can guide you in tweaking your content strategy to better serve your brand goals.

Finally, it's important to regularly evaluate and adjust your strategy to ensure continued alignment with your brand goals. Utilize analytics to track the performance of your videos and understand what resonates with your audience. This data-driven approach allows you to make informed decisions about future content and strategies, ensuring that your YouTube channel remains a powerful tool in achieving your brand's objectives.

In essence, aligning with brand goals is about creating a cohesive strategy that integrates your brand's mission with the dynamic, engaging platform that YouTube offers. It's about leveraging this powerful medium to not only reach but also resonate with your audience, ensuring that every interaction contributes to the larger narrative of your brand's success.

Chapter 3: Channel Branding Essentials

CRAFTING A UNIQUE CHANNEL NAME

Choosing the perfect name for your YouTube channel is not just an exercise in creativity; it is a strategic decision that can significantly impact your brand's visibility and memorability. Your channel name is often the first point of contact between your brand and potential subscribers. It sets the tone for your content and establishes the foundation of your brand identity. Therefore, investing time and thought into crafting a unique channel name is essential for setting your brand apart in the crowded digital landscape.

A compelling channel name should be distinctive and resonate with your target audience. Begin by considering the core values and mission of your brand. What message do you want to convey? What emotions or associations do you want your audience to have when they encounter your channel name? Reflecting on these questions can guide you toward a name that encapsulates the essence of your brand and creates a lasting impression.

Moreover, a unique channel name is crucial for searchability and discoverability on YouTube. With millions of channels vying for attention, a name that stands out can help potential viewers find your content more easily. Avoid generic or overly common names that may be lost in the sea of search results. Instead, aim for a name that is catchy, memorable, and easy to spell. This not only aids in search engine optimization (SEO) but also ensures that your audience can effortlessly recall and share your channel with others.

Consider incorporating keywords that are relevant to your niche or industry into your channel name. This can improve your channel's visibility in search results and attract viewers who are specifically interested in your content area. However, be cautious not to overload the name with keywords, as this can make it appear cluttered and detract from its appeal.

Another vital aspect is ensuring that your chosen name aligns with your brand's tone and personality. Whether your brand is professional, playful, or somewhere in between, your channel name should reflect this. Consistency in branding across all platforms, including YouTube, reinforces your brand identity and helps build trust with your audience.

Before finalizing your channel name, conduct thorough research to check its availability. Make sure the name is not already in use by another YouTube channel or brand. This prevents potential legal issues and confusion among viewers. Additionally, check for the availability of the corresponding domain name and social media handles. Having a consistent name across all platforms strengthens your brand's online presence and makes it easier for your audience to find you.

Remember, your YouTube channel name is more than just a label; it's a powerful tool that communicates your brand's story and draws your audience in. By thoughtfully crafting a unique and strategic channel name, you lay a solid foundation for your brand's success on YouTube. Invest the effort to get it right, and you'll be rewarded with a name that resonates with your audience, enhances your brand's visibility, and sets you on the path to achieving your online goals.

DESIGNING EYE-CATCHING LOGOS

Imagine scrolling through a sea of videos on YouTube. What makes you stop and click on a particular channel? More often than not, it's an eye-catching logo that seizes your attention. A logo is more than just a visual symbol; it's the face of your brand, the first impression that communicates your channel's essence to potential viewers. Designing a compelling logo is crucial for establishing a strong brand identity on YouTube.

The logo serves as a visual shorthand for your brand, encapsulating its values, mission, and personality in a single image. It's the anchor of your channel's visual identity, appearing on your profile, video thumbnails, and across social media platforms. With so much riding on this small graphic, investing time and creativity into the design process can significantly boost your channel's appeal and recognizability.

When designing a logo, clarity and simplicity should be at the forefront of your creative process. A logo must be easily recognizable and memorable, even at a glance. Overly complex designs can confuse viewers and dilute your brand's message. Instead, focus on clean lines, balanced compositions, and harmonious color schemes that reflect your brand's tone and content style.

Color psychology plays a pivotal role in logo design. Each color evokes specific emotions and associations. For example, red can convey passion and energy, while blue can suggest trust and professionalism. Consider what emotions you want your brand to evoke and choose your color palette accordingly. Consistency in color usage not only enhances brand cohesion but also aids in creating a lasting impression on your audience.

Typography is another crucial element. The font you choose should align with your brand's voice. A playful, informal font might suit a channel focused on entertainment, while a sleek, modern typeface could be ideal for tech-related content. Ensure that the typography is legible across various devices, as viewers will access your content on screens of all sizes.

Incorporating unique elements that resonate with your brand's niche can set your logo apart. This could be an icon, symbol, or stylized lettering that reflects the core of your content. These elements can subtly communicate your channel's focus, whether it's food, travel, education, or technology, helping potential subscribers understand what to expect from your videos.

Moreover, scalability is essential. Your logo should be versatile enough to look great in any size, from a tiny social media icon to a large banner. A scalable logo ensures that it maintains its integrity and recognizability regardless of where it's displayed.

Collaboration with a professional graphic designer can bring a fresh perspective and expertise to the table. If budget constraints are a concern, numerous online tools can assist in creating a polished logo. However, remember that your logo is an investment in your brand's future, and crafting a distinctive, high-quality design is worth the effort.

Ultimately, a well-designed logo not only attracts viewers but also fosters a sense of trust and professionalism. It tells your audience that your channel is worth their time, encouraging them to click, watch, and subscribe. In the competitive world of YouTube, an eye-catching logo is a powerful tool in building a successful and enduring brand.

CREATING CHANNEL ART

Imagine the moment when a potential subscriber lands on your YouTube channel. Within seconds, they assess whether your content aligns with their interests, and a significant part of their decision hinges on your channel art. This visual representation is not just a decorative element; it's the digital handshake that introduces your brand to the world. Crafting compelling channel art is crucial in establishing your brand's identity and enticing viewers to explore further.

Your channel art serves as the billboard for your brand. It's the first impression that communicates your brand's message, values, and personality. Therefore, it must be reflective of what your brand stands for. A well-designed banner can instantly convey professionalism, creativity, and credibility, which are essential in a crowded digital landscape. Consider it an opportunity to visually narrate your brand's story, showcasing what makes your content unique and worth subscribing to.

High-quality channel art also boosts brand recognition. When viewers see consistent visuals across your channel, videos, and social media platforms, they are more likely to remember your brand. This consistency builds trust and fosters a loyal audience. To achieve this, use colors, fonts, and imagery that align with your brand's overall aesthetic. These elements should be harmonized with your logo and any other brand assets to create a cohesive look.

It's crucial to remember that different devices display channel art differently. YouTube is accessed on various devices, from smartphones to large-screen TVs, and your channel art must look impeccable on all of them. The recommended size for YouTube channel art is 2560 x 1440 pixels, with the safe area being 1546 x 423 pixels. This ensures that your essential information and visuals are not cropped out on smaller screens. Utilizing templates can be beneficial in ensuring your design fits within these parameters.

Your channel art should also include essential information such as your upload schedule, social media handles, or a compelling call-to-action. This information not only helps in managing viewer expectations but also encourages them to connect with you on other platforms, expanding your brand's reach. However, balance is key; avoid cluttering your banner with too much text or imagery. The design should be clean and focused, allowing viewers to quickly grasp the key message.

Investing in professional design tools or hiring a graphic designer can elevate the quality of your channel art. Tools like Adobe Spark, Canva, or Snappa offer user-friendly platforms with templates specifically for YouTube channel art. These resources can help you create stunning visuals even if you lack extensive design skills.

In a world where viewers have countless options at their fingertips, your channel art can be the deciding factor in gaining a new subscriber. It is not just about aesthetics; it's about strategically communicating your brand's essence and inviting viewers to become part of your community. Remember, the right channel art doesn't just draw viewers in; it captivates them, making them eager to see what your brand has to offer.

WRITING A COMPELLING CHANNEL DESCRIPTION

Crafting a channel description that captivates and converts is an art form that every aspiring YouTube brand must master. The channel description is not merely a summary; it is the first impression you make on potential subscribers, and it serves as a pivotal tool in your brand's narrative. This is your opportunity to clearly convey your brand's purpose, values, and what viewers can expect from your content. A well-crafted description can be the difference between a casual visitor and a loyal subscriber.

Begin by understanding your target audience. What are their interests, challenges, and desires? Tailoring your description to resonate with these elements will make it more relatable and engaging. Use language that speaks directly to your audience, creating a sense of connection and understanding. By addressing their needs and demonstrating how your channel provides value, you establish a compelling reason for them to subscribe.

Clarity and conciseness are key. While it's important to be descriptive, avoid overwhelming your audience with lengthy paragraphs. Aim for a balance between informative and succinct. Highlight the core aspects of your channel: What topics do you cover? How frequently do you post? What makes your content unique? Answering these questions in a straightforward manner helps viewers immediately grasp what your channel is about.

Incorporate relevant keywords naturally throughout your description. This not only enhances the readability of your content but also optimizes it for search engines. Strategic keyword placement can improve your channel's visibility, making it easier for potential viewers to discover your content. However, ensure that the inclusion of keywords feels organic and does not detract from the overall flow of the text.

Don't forget to infuse your brand's personality into the description. Whether your channel is educational, entertaining, or inspirational, your tone should reflect your brand's identity. A consistent voice helps in building brand recognition and fosters a deeper connection with your audience. This is your chance to showcase what sets your brand apart, so be authentic and let your passion shine through.

Furthermore, include a call-to-action (CTA) to guide your viewers on what to do next. Whether it's subscribing to your channel, visiting your website, or following you on social media, a clear and compelling CTA can significantly enhance engagement. Encourage interaction and foster a sense of community, inviting viewers to become part of your brand's journey.

Lastly, periodically review and update your channel description. As your brand evolves, so too should your description. Keeping it current ensures that it accurately represents your brand and continues to attract the right audience. A dynamic description reflects an active and engaged channel, reinforcing your commitment to providing valuable content. By investing time and effort into crafting a compelling channel description, you lay a strong foundation for your YouTube brand's success.

Chapter 4: Producing High-Quality Videos

UNDERSTANDING VIDEO EQUIPMENT

In the digital age, where visual content reigns supreme, understanding video equipment is not just beneficial—it's essential for anyone serious about establishing a compelling YouTube presence for their brand. The right equipment can transform a simple idea into a powerful visual narrative that captivates audiences and amplifies brand identity across the platform. Investing in quality video equipment is not merely an expenditure; it is a strategic move that promises a substantial return in terms of audience engagement and brand loyalty.

The first step in this transformative journey is recognizing the impact of high-quality visuals. Viewers on YouTube are inundated with content, and only those videos that stand out with crisp, clear visuals and professional production values have a chance to capture and retain viewer attention. This is where understanding your equipment comes into play. A well-informed choice in cameras, lighting, and audio equipment can set the foundation for creating content that not only attracts viewers but also encourages them to subscribe and engage with your brand.

Cameras are the cornerstone of any video production setup. The market is flooded with various options, from DSLRs to mirrorless cameras, and even smartphones boasting impressive video capabilities. However, professional-grade cameras offer features like manual controls, interchangeable lenses, and superior image quality that are crucial for creating polished content. Understanding the technical specifications such as resolution, frame rate, and sensor size can significantly impact the final product, ensuring it meets the high standards expected by today's discerning viewers.

Lighting is another critical component that can dramatically affect the quality of your videos. Even the best cameras can produce mediocre results without proper lighting. Investing in a good set of lights—whether softboxes, ring lights, or LED panels—can elevate your video quality by ensuring consistent and flattering illumination. Understanding how to manipulate light can also help in setting the mood and tone of your videos, which is essential for aligning with your brand's message and aesthetic.

Audio quality often goes overlooked, yet it plays a pivotal role in maintaining viewer engagement. Poor audio can detract from even the most visually stunning content. Investing in high-quality microphones, such as lapel, shotgun, or condenser mics, can drastically improve your audio clarity, making your content more professional and enjoyable to watch. Understanding the basics of audio equipment and how to effectively integrate it into your setup is crucial for delivering a complete and immersive experience to your audience.

In addition to the primary equipment, accessories like tripods, gimbals, and editing software also contribute to the overall production quality. These tools help stabilize footage, add creative flair, and refine the final cut, ensuring that your videos not only meet but exceed audience expectations.

By understanding and investing in the right video equipment, you empower your brand to produce content that resonates with audiences and stands out in a crowded digital landscape. This strategic investment in quality and professionalism is the first step towards building a successful YouTube channel that not only showcases your brand's vision but also drives its growth and success.

MASTERING VIDEO EDITING

In the rapidly evolving digital landscape, video content has emerged as a dominant force, driving engagement and building communities. As you set up your YouTube channel for your brand, mastering video editing is not just an option but a necessity. The art of editing is where your vision comes to life, transforming raw footage into compelling narratives that resonate with your audience.

The power of video editing lies in its ability to enhance storytelling. Every cut, transition, and effect should serve a purpose, guiding viewers through your narrative with precision and flair. This process is not merely about assembling clips; it's about creating an experience. Your brand's story deserves to be told in a way that captures attention and sustains interest, and effective editing is your tool for achieving this.

Consider the impact of pacing. A well-edited video maintains a rhythm that keeps viewers engaged from start to finish. Whether it's fast-paced cuts that inject energy into a dynamic product showcase or slower transitions that allow for reflection and depth in a brand story, pacing is key. It dictates the emotional journey of your audience, making them feel exactly what you want them to feel at every moment.

Visual enhancements are another crucial aspect of video editing. Color grading, for instance, can drastically alter the mood of your content. A warm palette might evoke feelings of nostalgia or comfort, while cooler tones could suggest professionalism and modernity. These subtle adjustments speak volumes, reinforcing your brand's identity and message.

Moreover, sound design is an often underestimated yet powerful component of video editing. The right soundtrack can elevate your content, setting the tone and enhancing the emotional impact. Sound effects, when used strategically, can add layers of realism or highlight specific actions within your video. It's about creating an immersive experience that captivates your audience both visually and audibly.

Investing time in learning video editing software is crucial. Tools like Adobe Premiere Pro, Final Cut Pro, or DaVinci Resolve offer a plethora of features that can enhance your editing capabilities. While these programs may seem daunting initially, the payoff in terms of professionalism and polish is well worth the effort. Online tutorials and courses can provide guidance, helping you to harness these tools effectively.

The competitive nature of YouTube demands that your content not only stands out but also reflects the quality and values of your brand. Mastering video editing ensures that you present your brand in the best possible light, fostering a professional image that attracts and retains viewers. This skill empowers you to create videos that are not only informative but also aesthetically pleasing, aligning with the expectations of a discerning audience.

Ultimately, video editing is where creativity meets strategy. It's the bridge between concept and execution, where your brand's vision is meticulously crafted into a format that speaks to your audience. By mastering this skill, you position your brand for success, leveraging the full potential of video content to engage, inspire, and grow your community.

CREATING ENGAGING CONTENT

A successful YouTube channel thrives on the magnetism of its content. To captivate and retain your audience, the content must not only inform but also entertain and evoke emotion. Begin by understanding your target audience's desires and preferences. This understanding is the cornerstone of creating content that resonates. Engage in market research, analyze competitors, and immerse yourself in the cultural and social context of your audience. This will provide critical insights into what your viewers are seeking.

Next, focus on storytelling. Humans are naturally drawn to stories, and incorporating a narrative into your videos can significantly boost engagement. Whether you're demonstrating a product, sharing a testimonial, or providing a tutorial, weave a story that connects with your audience on a personal level. A strong narrative not only holds attention but also makes your content memorable.

Visuals are another powerful tool in your content creation arsenal. High-quality visuals can transform a mundane video into a captivating experience. Invest in good lighting, clear audio, and crisp video quality. Visual appeal is not just about aesthetics; it impacts the perceived credibility of your brand. Viewers are more likely to trust and engage with content that looks professional.

Interactivity is crucial. Encourage viewers to like, comment, and share your videos. Use calls to action effectively to guide your audience's engagement. Ask questions, prompt discussions, and create a community around your channel. This not only boosts engagement but also increases the likelihood of your content being shared, expanding your reach.

Consistency is key. Establish a regular posting schedule to keep your audience engaged and coming back for more. Consistency builds anticipation and loyalty. When viewers know when to expect new content, they are more likely to tune in regularly. This regular interaction strengthens the connection between your brand and your audience.

Additionally, embrace creativity and innovation. Experiment with different formats, styles, and themes. Whether it's trying out new editing techniques, incorporating animation, or exploring different content genres, innovation keeps your channel fresh and exciting. Don't be afraid to take risks and step outside of your comfort zone; it's often where the most engaging content is found.

Moreover, leverage the power of data analytics. Regularly review your channel's analytics to understand what content performs best, and why. This data-driven approach allows you to tailor your content strategy to better meet audience expectations and enhance engagement.

Finally, authenticity cannot be overstated. In a digital age saturated with content, authenticity stands out. Be genuine in your messaging and interactions. Authenticity builds trust and fosters a deeper connection with your audience, making them more likely to engage with your content and support your brand. By focusing on these strategies, you can create content that not only engages but also converts casual viewers into loyal supporters of your brand.

OPTIMIZING VIDEO LENGTH

In the fast-paced world of online content, capturing and retaining attention is crucial. When it comes to YouTube, video length is not merely a technical detail; it is a strategic tool that can significantly influence viewer engagement and channel growth. Crafting the optimal video length requires a balance between content depth and viewer retention, ensuring that each video serves its purpose without overstaying its welcome.

Understanding your audience is the first step in determining the ideal duration for your videos. Different demographics have varying preferences and attention spans, which means a one-size-fits-all approach is rarely effective. Analyze your target audience's behavior; younger viewers may prefer shorter, snappier content, while older demographics might appreciate more detailed, in-depth videos. Utilize YouTube Analytics to gain insights into viewer demographics and watch times, allowing you to tailor your content length to match their expectations.

The type of content you produce also plays a pivotal role in deciding video length. For instance, tutorials and educational content often benefit from longer formats that allow for comprehensive explanations and demonstrations. On the other hand, entertainment and lifestyle videos might thrive in shorter formats, where the focus is on delivering quick, engaging content that keeps the audience coming back for more. By aligning video length with content type, you ensure that the format enhances rather than detracts from the message.

Attention spans are dwindling in the digital age, and the first few seconds of your video are crucial in capturing interest. Hook your audience immediately with compelling intros and maintain their attention with a well-paced narrative. Avoid unnecessary filler that can lead to viewer drop-off. Every second should add value, whether through information, entertainment, or engagement. Remember, a concise and engaging video is more likely to be watched until the end, leading to better viewer retention rates and increased chances of your content being recommended by YouTube's algorithm.

Testing and iteration are key components in optimizing video length. Experiment with different durations and monitor viewer retention metrics to identify what works best for your channel. Pay attention to the audience retention graph in YouTube Analytics to see where viewers are dropping off, and adjust your content accordingly. This data-driven approach allows you to refine your strategy, ensuring that each video is as effective as possible in holding viewer interest.

Moreover, consider the platform's algorithmic preferences. YouTube favors videos that keep viewers on the platform longer, which means balancing viewer satisfaction with algorithmic visibility is essential. While longer videos can contribute to increased watch time, they must maintain high engagement levels to be beneficial. Striking this balance can enhance your channel's visibility and growth, making video length a critical factor in your YouTube strategy.

Ultimately, optimizing video length is about creating a seamless experience for your viewers. By understanding your audience, aligning content type with duration, and continuously refining your approach through analytics, you can craft videos that not only capture attention but also foster a loyal viewer base. The right video length can transform casual viewers into dedicated subscribers, driving your brand's success on YouTube.

Chapter 5: Optimizing for Search and Discovery

KEYWORD RESEARCH AND SEO

To truly harness the power of YouTube for your brand, understanding the pivotal role of keyword research and SEO is crucial. Imagine your YouTube channel as a vast library. In this library, keywords are the signposts that guide your audience to discover the valuable content you offer. Without these signposts, even the most engaging videos remain hidden in the shadows, unseen by the masses.

The first step in this transformative process is identifying the right keywords. These are the phrases and terms that your potential viewers are actively searching for. Think of them as the bridge connecting your content to the audience's needs and interests. By aligning your video content with these search terms, you increase the likelihood of your videos appearing in search results, thus increasing visibility and attracting more viewers.

To uncover these golden keywords, start by brainstorming a list of terms relevant to your brand and the topics you wish to cover. Next, utilize tools such as Google Keyword Planner,

TubeBuddy, or VidIQ. These platforms provide insights into search volume and competition levels, helping you refine your list to focus on terms that are both popular and attainable. Remember, targeting highly competitive keywords may require more effort to rank, so balancing between high volume and low competition is key.

Once you have your list of potential keywords, the next step is to seamlessly integrate them into your video strategy. This involves crafting compelling titles that incorporate your primary keyword naturally. A well-optimized title not only captures attention but also signals to YouTube's algorithm what your video is about. Similarly, the video description is another opportunity to embed keywords. A detailed and informative description not only aids in SEO but also provides viewers with a clear understanding of what to expect, encouraging longer watch times.

Tags are another essential element. They enhance discoverability by associating your video with related content. While tags hold less weight than titles and descriptions, they still play a role in the broader SEO strategy. Include a mix of broad and specific tags, ensuring they are relevant to the content.

Beyond text-based optimization, consider the impact of closed captions and transcripts. These elements make your content accessible to a broader audience, including those with hearing impairments or non-native speakers. Additionally, they provide an extra layer of text for search engines to crawl, further boosting your SEO efforts.

Consistency is also paramount. Regularly uploading content keeps your audience engaged and signals to YouTube that your channel is active, which can positively influence rankings. Monitor performance using YouTube Analytics to understand which keywords and content types resonate most with your audience. This data-driven approach allows you to refine your strategy continuously.

By investing time in keyword research and SEO, you lay a strong foundation for your YouTube channel. This strategic approach not only enhances visibility and reach but also positions your brand as an authority in your niche. With each video, you're not just sharing content; you're building a community and strengthening your brand's digital footprint.

CRAFTING EFFECTIVE TITLES AND DESCRIPTIONS

Imagine your YouTube channel as a bustling marketplace, filled with eager visitors searching for something that speaks to them. What draws them in? What makes them pause, intrigued, and willing to explore further? It's the promise of what they're about to experience, often encapsulated in the titles and descriptions of your videos. Crafting effective titles and descriptions is akin to being a skilled storyteller, where each word is carefully chosen to captivate and compel.

The title of your video is your first impression, the handshake that invites viewers into your world. It must be striking, clear, and infused with keywords that resonate with your audience's search queries. Think of your title as a beacon, guiding the right audience to your content amidst a sea of distractions. The key lies in balance: being descriptive enough to convey the essence of your content, yet succinct enough to maintain intrigue. Avoid misleading clickbait; instead, opt for authenticity that builds trust and encourages engagement.

Consider the psychology of curiosity. Humans are naturally drawn to the unknown, a powerful tool in your titling arsenal. Posing a question, hinting at a solution, or offering a surprising fact can spark curiosity. For instance, a title like "How to Boost Your Brand's Visibility in 24 Hours" immediately poses a challenge and promises a solution, compelling viewers to click.

Once your title has piqued interest, the description extends the invitation. It's your opportunity to provide a deeper understanding of what your video entails, setting expectations and enticing viewers to commit their time. Begin with a strong, captivating opening sentence that encapsulates the core message of your video. This is followed by a brief yet informative summary, enriched with keywords and phrases that align with your audience's interests and needs.

Descriptions also serve a dual purpose: engaging your audience and optimizing for search engines. YouTube's algorithm relies heavily on keywords to categorize and recommend content. Therefore, integrating relevant search terms naturally within your description not only enhances discoverability but also ensures that your content reaches those who are actively seeking it.

Moreover, the description is a space to foster connection and drive action. Encourage viewers to like, comment, and subscribe, creating a community around your brand. Include links to related content, your website, or social media platforms, guiding viewers to further engage with your brand.

Remember, crafting titles and descriptions is not a static process; it requires ongoing refinement and adaptation. Regularly analyze which titles and descriptions are performing well and use this data to inform future content strategies. Experiment with different approaches, learn from your audience's responses, and remain agile in your tactics.

Ultimately, the art of crafting effective titles and descriptions lies in your ability to understand and anticipate the needs and desires of your audience. By doing so, you transform your YouTube channel into a vibrant, magnetic space where your brand can thrive and connect meaningfully with its audience.

USING TAGS AND HASHTAGS

In the dynamic realm of YouTube, where content is king, ensuring your brand stands out requires more than just captivating videos. The strategic use of tags and hashtags is an indispensable tool in your digital arsenal. These elements are not mere accessories but rather powerful instruments that can propel your brand's visibility and audience engagement to unprecedented heights.

Tags and hashtags function as the connective tissue of your YouTube presence, seamlessly linking your content to relevant searches and similar videos. When used effectively, they enhance discoverability, enabling potential viewers to stumble upon your content amidst the sea of videos on the platform. This is crucial in an environment where millions of videos compete for attention every single day.

Consider tags as the keywords of your video content. They are the behind-the-scenes workers that inform YouTube's algorithm about the subject matter of your video. By selecting precise and relevant tags, you are essentially speaking the algorithm's language, guiding it to categorize and recommend your videos to users interested in similar topics. The choice of tags should be thoughtful and strategic, aligning with popular search terms without falling into the trap of mislabeling, which can harm your channel's credibility and performance.

On the other hand, hashtags are the public-facing identifiers that connect your content to trending topics and conversations. They serve as a bridge to broader discussions, allowing your brand to participate in and contribute to ongoing dialogues within your niche. This engagement can significantly amplify your reach and foster a sense of community among your viewers, who may be more inclined to interact with content that resonates with their interests.

To harness the full potential of tags and hashtags, one must adopt a systematic approach. Begin by researching popular and trending tags within your niche. Tools like Google Trends and YouTube's own search suggestions can offer valuable insights into what potential viewers are searching for. Analyze successful competitors and identify the tags they employ—this can provide a benchmark for your own strategy.

When it comes to hashtags, keep abreast of trending topics and current events that relate to your brand. However, it's important to strike a balance between relevance and reach. While it's tempting to use broad hashtags to capture a wider audience, niche-specific hashtags often yield more engaged and loyal viewers. Tailor your hashtags to align with both your content and audience's interests.

Moreover, consistency is key. Regularly update your tags and hashtags to reflect changes in your content strategy and shifts in viewer behavior. This adaptability ensures that your brand remains relevant and visible in an ever-evolving digital landscape.

Ultimately, the strategic use of tags and hashtags is about enhancing your brand's ability to connect with its desired audience. By mastering these tools, you can significantly boost your channel's reach, foster a deeper connection with your viewers, and cement your brand's presence on YouTube. The investment in understanding and implementing these elements will yield substantial returns in the form of increased visibility, engagement, and growth for your brand's YouTube channel.

CUSTOM THUMBNAILS FOR CLICK-THROUGH

In the vibrant world of YouTube, where countless creators compete for attention, the power of a compelling thumbnail cannot be overstated. Thumbnails are the first impression your potential viewers get, and they can mean the difference between a casual scroll past your video or a click that leads to a view. For brands seeking to establish a strong presence, custom thumbnails are an essential tool for boosting click-through rates and ensuring that your content stands out in the sea of digital noise.

Creating a custom thumbnail is not merely about slapping together a random image and some text. It is an art form that requires an understanding of your audience and what resonates with them. A well-designed thumbnail should capture the essence of your video content, offering a sneak peek that intrigues viewers and compels them to click. It should be visually appealing, with vibrant colors and clear, bold text that is easy to read even on small screens.

Consider the psychology of colors and how they can influence emotions and actions. Bright colors such as red, orange, and yellow are known to grab attention and can be used to highlight key elements in your thumbnail. However, it's important to maintain a balance and ensure that the thumbnail is not overwhelming or cluttered. Simplicity is key; a clean and organized design will convey professionalism and make your brand appear more trustworthy.

Text is another critical aspect of a successful thumbnail. It should be concise, conveying the main idea or a hook that piques curiosity. Ask a question, make a bold statement, or offer a compelling benefit that viewers can gain by watching your video. The font choice should align with your brand's identity, maintaining consistency across your channel, which helps in building brand recognition.

Images used in thumbnails should be high-quality and relevant to the video content. Faces, especially those expressing emotion, can be particularly effective in drawing in viewers as they naturally capture human interest. If your brand allows, incorporate your logo subtly into the thumbnail to reinforce brand visibility without overshadowing the main visual elements.

Testing and analyzing the performance of your thumbnails is crucial. YouTube provides analytics that can help you understand which thumbnails are performing best in terms of click-through rates. A/B testing different designs can provide insights into what works best for your audience, allowing you to optimize future thumbnails for maximum impact.

Incorporating custom thumbnails into your YouTube strategy is not just about increasing views; it's about building a cohesive and recognizable brand presence. When viewers recognize your brand through consistent and attractive thumbnails, they are more likely to become repeat viewers and subscribers, fostering a loyal audience base. As you refine your thumbnail strategy, remember that creativity, consistency, and audience understanding are your greatest allies in transforming casual viewers into engaged followers of your brand's YouTube channel.

Chapter 6: Building and Engaging Your Audience

PROMOTING YOUR CHANNEL

Imagine your YouTube channel as a thriving community, bustling with eager viewers and loyal subscribers, all excited to engage with your brand. The secret to achieving this lies in effective promotion. The digital marketplace is crowded, and standing out requires strategic efforts that go beyond merely uploading content. It's about creating a buzz, sparking curiosity, and encouraging viewers to become active participants in your brand's narrative.

First, leverage the power of social media. Your existing platforms such as Instagram, Twitter, Facebook, or LinkedIn are invaluable tools for promoting your YouTube channel. Share engaging snippets or teasers of your videos, use captivating visuals, and craft compelling captions that entice your audience to click through and watch the full content. Cross-promoting your videos on these platforms not only increases visibility but also taps into your existing follower base, turning them into subscribers.

In addition, consider collaborations with other YouTubers or influencers who share a similar audience demographic. Collaborations can introduce your channel to a wider audience and provide credibility through association. When viewers see a familiar face endorsing your content, they are more likely to trust and engage with it. This mutual exchange of audiences can significantly boost your subscriber count and expand your reach.

Optimize your video titles, descriptions, and tags with relevant keywords. This is crucial for search engine optimization (SEO), making it easier for potential viewers to discover your content. Think about what words or phrases your target audience might use to search for content like yours and incorporate them naturally into your video metadata. Remember, YouTube is the second largest search engine in the world, and utilizing SEO effectively can make a significant difference in how your channel is discovered.

Engagement is another powerful promotional tool. Interact with your audience by responding to comments, asking for feedback, and encouraging viewers to like, share, and subscribe. Building a community where viewers feel valued and heard can turn casual viewers into devoted fans. Additionally, by analyzing viewer feedback, you can tailor your content to better meet their interests and preferences, fostering a more engaged audience.

Don't underestimate the power of email marketing. If you have an email list, use it to your advantage by sending newsletters or updates about your latest YouTube videos. Provide a compelling reason for your subscribers to visit your channel, such as exclusive content or behind-the-scenes insights.

Lastly, consider investing in paid promotions. YouTube ads, Google Ads, or social media ads can help target specific demographics and increase your channel's visibility. While this requires a financial investment, it can be a highly effective way to attract new viewers and grow your audience quickly.

By employing these strategies, you can effectively promote your YouTube channel, transforming it from a hidden gem into a leading voice within your niche. Your brand's story deserves to be heard, and with the right promotional tactics, you can ensure it resonates far and wide. Engage with your audience, collaborate with peers, and strategically optimize your content to carve out a space for your brand in the bustling world of YouTube.

ENGAGING WITH COMMENTS AND FEEDBACK

In the vast digital landscape of YouTube, engaging with your audience through comments and feedback is not just an option—it is an essential strategy for building a thriving channel.

Every interaction in the comments section is an opportunity to foster community, gather insights, and amplify your brand's presence. By actively participating in these conversations, you demonstrate authenticity, which is crucial for establishing a loyal viewer base.

Imagine your YouTube channel as a bustling town square, where each comment is a passerby eager to share their thoughts. Acknowledging these voices not only makes them feel heard but also encourages further interaction. When viewers see that their opinions are valued, they are more likely to return, bringing with them a sense of belonging and loyalty to your brand. This dynamic creates a ripple effect, attracting even more engagement and extending your reach organically.

Responding to comments should be viewed as a dialogue rather than a monologue. This means engaging in meaningful conversations, asking questions, and providing thoughtful responses. This approach humanizes your brand, making it more relatable and approachable. Always aim to respond promptly and genuinely, as this shows that you are attentive and appreciative of your audience's input. Even a simple 'thank you' can go a long way in building goodwill and trust.

Feedback, whether positive or negative, is a treasure trove of insights. Positive comments can highlight what resonates with your audience, guiding you to create more of what they love. Negative feedback, on the other hand, should not be shunned but embraced as constructive criticism. It provides invaluable information on areas that may need improvement, helping you refine your content strategy. Addressing criticism with grace and a willingness to improve can turn potential detractors into loyal supporters.

Furthermore, leveraging comments and feedback as a source of content inspiration can keep your channel fresh and relevant. Pay attention to recurring themes or questions in your comments section. These can serve as the foundation for future videos, ensuring that your content remains aligned with your audience's interests and needs. By doing so, you not only demonstrate that you are attentive to your audience but also that you are committed to delivering value.

To streamline this process, consider using tools and features that YouTube provides, such as pinning insightful comments or using the heart feature to highlight valuable contributions. These features can help you manage engagement efficiently while ensuring important interactions are visible to all viewers.

Engaging with comments and feedback is not just about maintaining a presence; it is about creating a vibrant community centered around your brand. This community becomes a powerful extension of your marketing efforts, as satisfied viewers often become brand advocates who share your content with others. By nurturing these relationships, you lay the groundwork for sustained growth and success on YouTube. Actively engaging with your audience is a strategic investment in the longevity and impact of your brand's digital footprint. Embrace this opportunity to connect, learn, and evolve alongside your audience, ensuring that your YouTube channel remains a dynamic and influential platform.

COLLABORATIONS AND CROSS-PROMOTIONS

Imagine tapping into a network that already possesses a substantial following, eager and ready to engage with new content. This is what collaborations and cross-promotions offer to your YouTube channel. By strategically partnering with other creators or brands, you can significantly boost your visibility and reach audiences that might otherwise remain elusive. These partnerships are not just about increasing numbers; they are about building a community and creating content that resonates on a larger scale.

Collaborating with others in your niche or complementary sectors can provide a fresh perspective and introduce your brand to diverse audiences. When choosing partners, it's crucial to ensure their values and content style align with your brand's ethos. This alignment ensures authenticity, which audiences can easily detect and appreciate. Authentic collaborations foster trust and loyalty, encouraging viewers to explore your channel further.

The art of cross-promotion lies in its mutual benefits. Both parties can share audiences, increasing subscribers and engagement. For instance, if you are a beauty brand, collaborating with a fashion influencer can introduce your products to fashion enthusiasts who might also be interested in beauty tips. This synergy not only broadens your audience but also enhances the value of the content provided to viewers, making it a win-win situation.

Organizing collaborative content can take various forms. It could be a joint video series, a guest appearance, or even a takeover where a collaborator manages your channel for a day. These formats keep your content fresh and exciting, drawing in viewers who are curious about the new dynamics. Furthermore, cross-promotions can extend beyond YouTube. Utilizing other platforms such as Instagram, TikTok, or a blog can amplify your reach, creating a cohesive and comprehensive promotional strategy.

To initiate a successful collaboration, start by reaching out to potential partners with a clear proposal. Highlight the benefits of the partnership and outline how it can be mutually advantageous. Personalize your approach by referencing specific content of theirs that aligns with your brand, demonstrating genuine interest and understanding of their work.

Once a collaboration is set, promote it extensively. Utilize teasers, countdowns, and behind-the-scenes content to build anticipation. Engage with your audience through comments and community posts, encouraging them to participate and share their thoughts. This engagement not only increases visibility but also strengthens the bond with your audience.

Measure the success of your collaborations through metrics such as subscriber growth, engagement rates, and viewer feedback. These insights can guide future partnerships and refine your approach, ensuring each collaboration is more impactful than the last.

By embracing collaborations and cross-promotions, you are not just enhancing your subscriber count but also enriching your content and fostering a community. These partnerships are a testament to the power of connectivity in the digital age, proving that when brands unite, they can achieve remarkable heights.

BUILDING A COMMUNITY

Creating a YouTube channel for your brand is not just about uploading videos; it's about building a thriving community that rallies around your content, shares your values, and amplifies your message. The power of a community lies in its ability to transform passive viewers into active participants who are invested in your brand's journey. To build such a community, engagement, authenticity, and value must be at the forefront of your strategy.

Firstly, engagement is the cornerstone of community building. It is not enough to simply post content and hope for interaction. Actively encourage your viewers to participate in the conversation by asking questions, responding to comments, and creating content that invites dialogue. Host live streams where you can interact in real-time, allowing your audience to feel seen and heard. Foster a sense of belonging by acknowledging your viewers' contributions, whether through shout-outs, featuring their comments in your videos, or creating content based on their suggestions. This two-way communication establishes a connection that goes beyond the screen.

Authenticity is another critical element in building a community. In a world saturated with content, viewers are drawn to creators who are genuine and relatable. Share your brand's story, mission, and values openly. Let your audience see the human side of your brand by showcasing behind-the-scenes content, sharing personal anecdotes, or discussing challenges and triumphs. This transparency builds trust and loyalty, as viewers feel they are part of a community that values honesty and integrity.

Providing value is essential to keep your community engaged and growing. Your content should not only entertain but also educate or inspire your audience. Identify what your viewers are passionate about or what problems they need solving, and tailor your content to meet these needs. Whether it's through tutorials, tips, motivational talks, or industry insights, consistently delivering valuable content will encourage your audience to return and recommend your channel to others.

Moreover, leverage the power of social media to extend your community beyond YouTube. Establish a presence on platforms where your audience is active, and use these channels to promote your content, share updates, and engage with your community. Create a dedicated space, such as a Facebook group or Discord server, where your audience can connect with each other. This not only strengthens the community but also allows for deeper engagement and collaboration among members.

Building a community around your YouTube channel is a deliberate and ongoing process. It requires dedication, patience, and a genuine desire to connect with your audience. By focusing on engagement, authenticity, and value, you can cultivate a loyal community that supports your brand and contributes to its growth. Remember, a strong community is not just a group of viewers; it's a network of advocates who believe in your brand and are excited to be part of its evolution.

Chapter 7: Monetizing Your YouTube Channel

UNDERSTANDING YOUTUBE PARTNER PROGRAM

Imagine transforming your brand into a household name, reaching millions of potential customers worldwide, and generating a steady stream of income—all from the comfort of your own home. This is not just a dream; it's a reality that thousands of brands are achieving every day through the YouTube Partner Program. As you set up your YouTube channel, understanding the nuances of this program becomes crucial to unlocking its full potential for your brand.

The YouTube Partner Program is not merely a feature; it's a gateway to monetization, offering a plethora of opportunities to turn your creative content into a profitable venture. It provides you with the tools and resources necessary to monetize your videos and grow your brand's presence in the digital landscape. By tapping into this program, you can leverage YouTube's vast audience, which spans across demographics and geographical boundaries, to promote your brand effectively.

To become part of this lucrative program, there are essential eligibility criteria that your channel must meet. These include having at least 1,000 subscribers and 4,000 watch hours within the past 12 months. While these numbers might seem daunting at first, they serve as a benchmark to ensure that your content resonates with viewers and maintains a consistent level of quality and engagement. Meeting these requirements is a testament to your brand's potential to captivate and grow an audience.

Once eligible, the YouTube Partner Program opens up a variety of monetization options. These include ad revenue from display, overlay, and video ads, which are tailored by YouTube to suit your audience's interests, ensuring maximum engagement and return on investment. Additionally, you can explore channel memberships, where loyal viewers pay a monthly fee for exclusive content, and merchandise shelf, allowing you to sell branded merchandise directly from your channel. These monetization strategies provide multiple revenue streams, each offering a unique way to engage with your audience and enhance your brand's value.

Moreover, the program offers access to advanced features like YouTube Analytics, which provides invaluable insights into viewer demographics, traffic sources, and engagement metrics. This data-driven approach allows you to refine your content strategy, optimize your videos for better performance, and ultimately, grow your channel more efficiently. By understanding your audience's preferences and behaviors, you can tailor your content to meet their needs, ensuring sustained growth and success.

Participating in the YouTube Partner Program also means joining a community of creators who are passionate about their craft and committed to supporting each other's growth. This community offers opportunities for collaboration, cross-promotion, and learning, fostering an environment that encourages creativity and innovation. By engaging with fellow creators, you can exchange ideas, share experiences, and build valuable relationships that can propel your brand forward.

In essence, the YouTube Partner Program is not just about monetization; it's about strategically positioning your brand in the digital marketplace. It's about harnessing the power of video content to build a loyal audience, enhance your brand's visibility, and achieve your business objectives. By understanding and leveraging this program, you can transform your YouTube channel into a powerful marketing tool that drives growth and success for your brand.

EXPLORING AD REVENUE

Imagine tapping into a stream of revenue that flows effortlessly while you sleep, all by leveraging the power of your brand's YouTube channel. Ad revenue is a potent tool that can transform your channel from a simple communication platform into a dynamic income-generating engine. YouTube's vast audience and sophisticated ad placement algorithms offer an unparalleled opportunity to monetize your content effectively. To harness this potential, understanding and optimizing ad revenue streams is crucial.

The first step to unlocking ad revenue is to become a YouTube Partner. This partnership opens the door to YouTube's monetization features, allowing you to earn money from ads displayed on your videos. To qualify, your channel needs to meet specific criteria: a minimum of 1,000 subscribers and 4,000 watch hours in the past 12 months. Achieving these benchmarks not only signifies audience engagement but also positions your brand as a credible content creator.

Once you join the YouTube Partner Program, you can start earning through different types of ads. Skippable video ads, non-skippable video ads, display ads, overlay ads, and bumper ads each have unique characteristics and benefits. Skippable ads are popular among advertisers because they only pay when viewers watch the ad for at least 30 seconds. Non-skippable ads, although potentially more intrusive, can be more lucrative as they guarantee full viewer attention. Understanding these ad types and strategically placing them in your content can significantly impact your revenue.

To maximize ad revenue, it's essential to create content that attracts advertisers willing to pay a premium to reach your audience. Focus on producing high-quality, engaging videos that keep viewers watching longer. The more watch time your videos accumulate, the more ad impressions you can generate, thereby increasing your potential earnings. Additionally, maintaining a consistent posting schedule can help build a loyal audience and improve your channel's algorithmic favorability, further boosting your revenue potential.

Another critical factor in increasing ad revenue is optimizing your channel for search and discovery. Utilize relevant keywords in your titles, descriptions, and tags to improve your videos' visibility. A well-optimized channel attracts more viewers, which translates to higher watch times and more ad impressions. Furthermore, engaging with your audience through comments and social media can enhance viewer retention and foster a community around your brand, making your channel more attractive to advertisers.

Diversifying your content can also attract a broader audience and increase ad revenue. Experiment with different video formats, such as tutorials, vlogs, or interviews, to see what resonates best with your viewers. By diversifying, you not only maintain viewer interest but also open up opportunities for different types of ads and sponsorships.

Lastly, regularly analyzing your channel's performance through YouTube Analytics is crucial. This tool provides insights into which videos are generating the most revenue, allowing you to fine-tune your content strategy. By understanding your audience demographics and viewing habits, you can tailor your content to maximize engagement and ad revenue.

Ad revenue is not just an additional income stream; it is a fundamental component of a successful YouTube strategy. By strategically optimizing your content and channel, you can turn your brand's YouTube presence into a profitable venture, ensuring your brand thrives in the digital landscape.

UTILIZING SPONSORED CONTENT

In the bustling world of YouTube, where millions of videos vie for attention, leveraging sponsored content can be a powerful strategy to elevate your brand's presence. Sponsored content not only provides financial support but also enhances credibility and expands reach. By collaborating with sponsors who align with your brand values, you create a symbiotic relationship that benefits both parties and captivates your audience.

When considering sponsored content, it is essential to identify potential sponsors whose products or services complement your brand. This alignment ensures authenticity, which is crucial in maintaining the trust of your audience. A well-matched sponsor can enhance your content by providing resources, ideas, or unique insights that resonate with your viewers.

Crafting compelling sponsored content requires a delicate balance between promotion and genuine engagement. The content should seamlessly integrate the sponsor's message without overshadowing your brand's voice. Transparency is key; clearly disclose any sponsorships to maintain the trust and integrity of your relationship with your audience. This honesty fosters a sense of community and respect, encouraging viewers to engage more deeply with your content.

To maximize the effectiveness of sponsored content, consider creative formats that capture attention and encourage interaction. Whether it's a product review, a tutorial, or a behind-the-scenes look, the content should be engaging and informative. Utilize storytelling to weave the sponsor's message into a narrative that resonates with your audience. This approach not only highlights the sponsor's offerings but also enriches the viewing experience, making it memorable and impactful.

Furthermore, it's important to evaluate the performance of your sponsored content. Utilize YouTube's analytics tools to assess viewer engagement, retention rates, and feedback. This data provides valuable insights into what resonates with your audience and what can be improved. Engage with your community by encouraging feedback and responding to comments, fostering a dialogue that can lead to further collaboration opportunities.

Building long-term relationships with sponsors can be highly beneficial. Consistent partnerships allow for more cohesive content planning and execution, creating a reliable source of support for your channel. These relationships can evolve into collaborations that extend beyond YouTube, opening up new avenues for brand visibility and growth.

Incorporating sponsored content into your YouTube strategy requires careful planning and execution. By selecting the right partners and crafting authentic, engaging content, you can create a dynamic channel that not only entertains but also educates and inspires. Sponsored content, when utilized effectively, becomes a valuable tool in your brand's growth arsenal, driving success and fostering a loyal, engaged community.

DIVERSIFYING INCOME STREAMS

Imagine transforming your YouTube channel into a dynamic hub that not only builds your brand but also becomes a powerful engine for generating revenue. While many creators focus solely on ad revenue, there is a vast landscape of opportunities waiting to be explored. By diversifying your income streams, you can unlock the full potential of your YouTube channel and secure financial stability for your brand.

One of the most compelling ways to diversify income is through sponsorships and brand partnerships. As your channel grows and your audience becomes more engaged, brands will naturally gravitate towards you for collaboration. These partnerships can be incredibly lucrative, providing a steady stream of income while also enhancing your brand's credibility. It's important to choose partnerships that align with your brand values, ensuring authenticity and maintaining the trust of your audience.

Another lucrative avenue is merchandise. If your brand has a strong, recognizable identity, consider launching a line of branded products. From apparel to accessories, merchandise allows your audience to become ambassadors for your brand, all while generating additional revenue. Platforms like Teespring or Spreadshop make it easy to design and sell merchandise without the need for upfront investment.

Affiliate marketing also presents a fantastic opportunity for income diversification. By recommending products or services that are relevant to your audience, you can earn a commission on each sale made through your referral links. This strategy not only provides value to your audience by introducing them to products they may find useful but also generates a passive income stream for your brand.

For those with expertise in a particular field, offering online courses or workshops can be highly profitable. By leveraging your knowledge, you can create valuable content that your audience is willing to pay for. Platforms like Teachable or Udemy provide a user-friendly way to design and sell courses, allowing you to monetize your expertise while building a community of engaged learners.

Memberships and subscription models are also gaining traction as effective ways to diversify income. By offering exclusive content, early access to videos, or behind-the-scenes insights, you can provide additional value to your most dedicated followers. Platforms like Patreon or YouTube's own membership feature make it easy to set up a subscription model, providing a reliable monthly income stream.

Moreover, live events and webinars can be a fantastic source of revenue while deepening your connection with your audience. Whether it's a virtual Q&A session or a live demonstration, these events offer a unique opportunity to interact with your audience in real-time. Charging a small fee for access can generate income while providing a memorable experience for your viewers.

In a rapidly evolving digital landscape, relying on a single income stream can be risky. By embracing a multifaceted approach to monetization, you not only safeguard your brand against market fluctuations but also create a more resilient business model. Each income stream enhances your brand's value proposition, offering your audience diverse ways to engage and support your channel. Now is the time to explore these opportunities and elevate your YouTube channel to new heights.

Chapter 8: Analyzing and Improving Performance

USING YOUTUBE ANALYTICS

Imagine harnessing a powerful tool that not only tracks the performance of your YouTube channel but also provides actionable insights to elevate your brand's presence. YouTube Analytics is that tool, and it is indispensable for anyone serious about maximizing their channel's impact. By leveraging the vast array of data available through YouTube Analytics, you can transform your channel into a strategic asset that drives brand growth and audience engagement.

The first step to utilizing YouTube Analytics is understanding its metrics, which serve as the foundation for informed decision-making. Key metrics such as watch time, average view duration, and audience retention give you a clear picture of how your content resonates with viewers. These insights allow you to tailor your content to meet the preferences of your audience, ensuring that each video not only captures attention but also holds it.

Moreover, YouTube Analytics provides detailed demographics, offering a window into who your viewers are. This information is crucial for aligning your content with the interests and needs of your target audience. Whether it's age, gender, or geographic location, these demographic insights can guide your content strategy, ensuring it is both relevant and engaging to those you aim to reach.

Another powerful feature of YouTube Analytics is traffic source analysis. Understanding where your viewers are coming from—be it search, suggested videos, or external links—enables you to optimize your promotional efforts. By focusing on the most productive traffic sources, you can enhance your channel's visibility and attract a larger, more engaged audience.

Engagement metrics such as likes, comments, and shares provide a direct line to your audience's sentiments. These interactions are not just numbers; they are feedback that can guide your content creation. Encouraging viewer engagement through calls-to-action and responding to comments can foster a community around your brand, turning passive viewers into active participants.

Furthermore, YouTube Analytics offers insights into your revenue streams if your channel is monetized. By analyzing metrics related to ad performance, you can identify which content generates the most revenue and explore opportunities to increase your earnings. This financial perspective is invaluable for sustaining and growing your channel as a viable business asset.

To fully capitalize on YouTube Analytics, consistency in monitoring and evaluating your metrics is key. Regular analysis allows you to track your progress over time, identify trends, and adjust your strategies accordingly. This proactive approach ensures that your channel remains dynamic and responsive to the ever-evolving digital landscape.

In essence, YouTube Analytics is not just a tool—it's a strategic partner in your brand's journey to success. By delving into the wealth of data at your disposal, you can craft a channel that not only reflects your brand's essence but also captivates and grows your audience. Embrace the power of analytics, and unlock the full potential of your YouTube channel as a formidable force in your brand's digital strategy.

TRACKING KEY METRICS

In the ever-evolving landscape of digital marketing, establishing a YouTube channel for your brand is only the beginning. The real work lies in understanding the performance of your content and making informed decisions to enhance your brand's visibility and engagement. Tracking key metrics is not just an option—it's an essential practice for any brand serious about thriving in the competitive world of online video content.

To truly harness the power of YouTube, you need to delve into the analytics that the platform offers. YouTube Analytics provides a wealth of information that is crucial for understanding how your audience interacts with your content. By examining these metrics, you can gain insights into viewer behavior, identify trends, and tailor your content strategy to better meet the needs and preferences of your audience.

One of the most important metrics to consider is watch time. Watch time is a comprehensive measure that reflects the total minutes viewers spend watching your videos. A higher watch time indicates that your content is engaging and retains viewer attention, which is a strong signal to YouTube's algorithm to promote your videos more widely. Therefore, focusing on creating compelling content that encourages viewers to watch longer can significantly boost your channel's visibility.

Another critical metric is audience retention, which shows the percentage of a video that viewers watch before clicking away. This metric helps you pinpoint the exact moments when viewers lose interest, allowing you to adjust video length, pacing, and content to keep your audience engaged throughout. By analyzing audience retention, you can refine your video structure and improve viewer satisfaction.

Engagement metrics such as likes, comments, and shares are also vital indicators of how your content resonates with your audience. These interactions not only enhance your video's visibility through YouTube's algorithm but also foster a sense of community around your brand. Encouraging viewers to like, comment, and share your videos can amplify your reach and strengthen your connection with your audience.

Subscriber growth is another key metric that reflects the health of your channel. A steady increase in subscribers indicates that viewers find value in your content and are interested in receiving more. Tracking subscriber growth over time can help you identify which types of content are most effective in attracting and retaining an audience, allowing you to optimize your content strategy accordingly.

In addition to these metrics, it's important to pay attention to traffic sources. Understanding where your viewers are coming from—whether it's YouTube search, suggested videos, or external websites—can inform your promotional strategies and highlight opportunities for collaboration and cross-promotion.

By regularly monitoring these key metrics, you can make data-driven decisions that enhance your channel's performance and elevate your brand's presence on YouTube. The insights gained from tracking these metrics empower you to refine your content, engage with your audience more effectively, and ultimately achieve your brand's goals in the digital space. Embrace the power of analytics, and let the data guide your journey to YouTube success.

IDENTIFYING GROWTH OPPORTUNITIES

In the ever-evolving landscape of digital marketing, identifying growth opportunities for your YouTube channel is akin to discovering hidden treasures that propel your brand to new heights. The key to unlocking these opportunities lies in a strategic analysis of your current standing, audience engagement, and market trends. By delving into these aspects, you can uncover the potential pathways that lead to exponential growth and increased brand visibility.

First, conduct a thorough audit of your existing content and channel performance. Analyze metrics such as view counts, watch time, audience retention, and subscriber growth. These data points provide invaluable insights into what resonates with your audience and what falls flat. By understanding which videos drive the most engagement, you can tailor future content to match your audience's preferences, thereby maximizing your channel's potential for growth.

Next, consider the untapped potential within your current audience. Engage with your viewers through comments, community posts, and social media interactions to gain insights into their needs and interests. By fostering a community-centric approach, you not only build loyalty but also gather critical information that can guide your content strategy. Encourage feedback and be open to suggestions, as your audience can often point you toward lucrative niches or content ideas that you may have overlooked.

Another crucial aspect of identifying growth opportunities is staying abreast of the latest trends in your industry. YouTube is a dynamic platform where trends can shift rapidly, and staying ahead of the curve can give you a competitive edge. Regularly monitor industry news, popular channels within your niche, and trending topics on YouTube to identify emerging themes and content formats. Adapting your content strategy to incorporate these trends can attract a wider audience and position your brand as a thought leader in your field.

Collaborations and partnerships also present significant growth opportunities. By teaming up with other content creators or brands that share a similar audience, you can tap into their viewer base and introduce your channel to potential subscribers. Look for creators whose content complements your own and propose mutually beneficial collaborations. Whether it's a joint video, guest appearances, or cross-promotions, these partnerships can significantly expand your reach and enhance your brand's credibility.

Furthermore, consider diversifying your content offerings to cater to different segments of your audience. Experiment with various content types such as tutorials, vlogs, interviews, or live streams to see what garners the most engagement. Diversification not only keeps your content fresh and engaging but also attracts different audience demographics, increasing your channel's overall appeal.

Lastly, invest in optimizing your channel for search and discovery. Utilize SEO best practices by including relevant keywords in your video titles, descriptions, and tags. Create eye-catching thumbnails and compelling video intros to capture viewers' attention and encourage click-throughs. By enhancing your channel's discoverability, you can attract organic traffic and grow your subscriber base.

In the quest for growth, it is imperative to remain adaptable and receptive to change. By continuously evaluating your strategies and remaining vigilant for new opportunities, you can ensure that your YouTube channel not only thrives but becomes an integral part of your brand's success story.

ITERATING BASED ON FEEDBACK

Launching a YouTube channel for your brand is only the beginning of a dynamic and evolving process. As with any successful venture, the key to long-term growth and improvement lies in embracing feedback and using it to refine your strategy. Feedback is a goldmine of insights that can inform every aspect of your content strategy, from the type of videos you produce to the way you engage with your audience. By actively listening to your viewers and understanding their needs and preferences, you can ensure that your channel remains relevant and appealing.

One of the most effective ways to gather feedback is through the comments section of your videos. This space is where your audience shares their thoughts, reactions, and suggestions. It is crucial to engage with these comments, respond to questions, and acknowledge constructive criticism. This not only builds a sense of community but also provides you with direct insight into what your audience values. Pay close attention to recurring themes and suggestions, as these can highlight areas for potential improvement or new content ideas.

Analytics tools provided by YouTube are another invaluable resource. They offer detailed data on viewer behavior, such as watch time, audience retention, and demographic information.

By analyzing this data, you can identify which videos are performing well and which are not. Look for patterns in the types of content that generate the most engagement and consider how you can expand on these successful elements. Additionally, low retention rates might indicate that your videos need to be more engaging or shorter in length to maintain interest.

Surveys and polls can also be an effective method for gathering feedback. Utilize YouTube's community tab or external platforms to ask your audience directly about their preferences and expectations. Questions could range from topics they want to see covered to preferred video lengths or styles. This proactive approach not only provides you with valuable data but also demonstrates to your audience that you value their input and are committed to delivering content that meets their needs.

Experimentation is another critical component of iterating based on feedback. Use the insights gained from comments, analytics, and surveys to test new ideas and formats. Don't be afraid to try something different, whether it's a new video series, a change in presentation style, or incorporating different types of media. Monitor the response to these changes closely, and be prepared to adapt quickly. Iteration is not about making one-time changes but about continuously evolving and improving.

Lastly, remember that feedback can also come from within your team or collaborators. Encourage open discussions about what's working and what isn't. Different perspectives can provide fresh insights and help identify blind spots. Regularly reviewing your channel's performance as a team ensures that everyone is aligned and working towards the same goals.

Incorporating feedback into your YouTube strategy is not a one-off task but an ongoing process. It requires an open mind, a willingness to adapt, and a commitment to excellence. By making iterative improvements based on feedback, you can create a channel that not only grows in popularity but also fosters a loyal and engaged community.

Chapter 9: Navigating Legal and Ethical Considerations

UNDERSTANDING COPYRIGHT LAWS

In the digital age, understanding copyright laws is not merely a legal obligation; it is a strategic necessity for anyone aiming to establish a successful YouTube channel for their brand. As creators, the content we produce becomes a powerful asset, but it also subjects us to a complex web of legal considerations. Comprehending these laws can be the difference between a flourishing channel and one plagued by legal disputes, which could potentially tarnish your brand's reputation.

Copyright laws are designed to protect the intellectual property rights of creators, ensuring that their original works are not used without permission. This protection extends to everything from videos and music to images and text. As a brand establishing a presence on YouTube, it is critical to recognize that any content you use that is not originally yours may be subject to copyright protection. Ignorance is not a defense in the eyes of the law, and infringing on someone else's intellectual property can lead to severe consequences, including fines, channel suspension, or even lawsuits.

One of the most common pitfalls for YouTube creators is the use of copyrighted music. Including a popular song in your video might seem harmless, but without proper licensing, it constitutes a copyright violation. YouTube's Content ID system is designed to detect such infringements and can automatically flag or remove your video, impacting your channel's standing. Opting for royalty-free music or obtaining proper licenses for copyrighted tracks ensures your content remains compliant and avoids any disruptions.

Visual content is another area where many creators falter. Using images or video clips that you do not own or have not licensed can lead to copyright claims. Even if the content is readily available online, it does not mean it is free for public use. Investing in stock footage or creating original visuals can safeguard your brand from potential legal issues.

Moreover, the concept of 'Fair Use' often confuses creators. While it allows limited use of copyrighted material without permission, its application is nuanced and varies by jurisdiction. Factors such as the purpose of use, the nature of the copyrighted work, the amount used, and the effect on the market value are considered when determining fair use. Misinterpreting these factors can lead to costly mistakes.

To protect your brand and uphold the integrity of your YouTube channel, it is essential to develop a robust understanding of copyright laws. This involves not only recognizing what constitutes a copyright infringement but also implementing strategies to avoid them. Educating yourself and your team, seeking legal advice when necessary, and using resources like YouTube's Creator Academy can fortify your channel against potential legal challenges.

Ultimately, respecting copyright laws reflects your brand's commitment to ethical practices. It builds trust with your audience, who will appreciate the originality and legitimacy of your content. By prioritizing compliance, you pave the way for sustainable growth and success on YouTube, ensuring your brand's creative vision is realized without legal hindrances. In this competitive digital landscape, understanding and adhering to copyright laws is not just an option; it is an imperative.

ENSURING COMPLIANCE WITH YOUTUBE POLICIES

Navigating the expansive world of YouTube offers unparalleled opportunities for brand visibility, but with great opportunity comes the responsibility of adhering to YouTube's comprehensive policies. Ensuring compliance with these guidelines is not merely a legal obligation but a strategic move that can safeguard your brand's reputation and foster trust with your audience. Let's delve into why prioritizing compliance is not just beneficial but essential for your brand's success on YouTube.

First, consider the implications of non-compliance. YouTube's algorithms are adept at identifying and flagging content that violates its community guidelines. This can lead to videos being demonetized, removed, or even result in strikes against your channel. Accumulating strikes can culminate in the suspension or permanent deletion of your channel, a devastating blow to any brand seeking to establish a lasting presence on the platform. By ensuring compliance, you not only avoid these penalties but also present your brand as one that respects and adheres to community standards.

Moreover, YouTube policies are designed to create a safe and respectful environment for all users. Adhering to these policies demonstrates your brand's commitment to ethical practices and respect for your audience. This commitment is crucial in building a loyal community that trusts and values your content. When audiences perceive a brand as trustworthy and respectful, they are more likely to engage with and advocate for that brand, leading to increased reach and influence.

Additionally, compliance with YouTube's policies enhances your brand's credibility. In an age where content is abundant, credibility is a key differentiator. A brand that consistently follows platform guidelines is more likely to be viewed as professional and reliable. This perception can be a significant advantage, particularly when competing for attention in a crowded digital landscape.

Furthermore, understanding and adhering to YouTube's policies can provide insights into content creation that aligns with audience expectations and platform standards. This alignment not only helps in avoiding content removal but also optimizes your content for better performance on the platform. YouTube's algorithm favors content that adheres to its guidelines, which can lead to higher visibility and engagement. Compliance, therefore, can be a catalyst for growth, driving traffic and increasing your brand's visibility.

Lastly, embracing compliance is an opportunity to innovate within the framework of YouTube's policies. Creativity thrives within constraints, and understanding the boundaries set by YouTube can inspire unique and engaging content that resonates with your audience while adhering to the rules. By viewing compliance as a catalyst for creativity rather than a hindrance, your brand can produce content that is both impactful and policy-compliant.

In essence, ensuring compliance with YouTube policies is an investment in your brand's long-term success on the platform. It protects your channel from potential pitfalls, fosters trust and credibility, and opens new avenues for creative expression. By prioritizing compliance, your brand not only aligns with YouTube's standards but also sets the stage for sustainable growth and influence in the digital realm.

HANDLING NEGATIVE FEEDBACK

In the dynamic world of YouTube, feedback is the lifeblood of growth and innovation. However, not all feedback is positive, and it's crucial for brands to harness the potential of negative feedback to refine their message and strengthen their community. Understanding how to effectively manage and respond to criticism can transform challenges into opportunities for improvement and connection with your audience.

First and foremost, it's important to approach negative feedback with an open mind and a calm demeanor. Emotional responses can cloud judgment and hinder constructive engagement. By maintaining a professional and courteous stance, you can demonstrate maturity and dedication to your audience's concerns. This not only helps in defusing potentially heated situations but also showcases your brand's commitment to transparency and improvement.

Moreover, negative feedback often contains valuable insights that can lead to meaningful advancements in your content strategy. View each criticism as a potential source of information that can help you understand your audience better. Analyze the feedback to identify patterns or recurring themes that might indicate areas needing attention or enhancement. This analytical approach can be a powerful tool in guiding content adjustments and enhancing overall viewer satisfaction.

Engagement is key when dealing with negative feedback. Respond promptly and thoughtfully to comments, showing that you value your audience's input and are willing to engage in dialogue. A well-crafted response can turn a dissatisfied viewer into a loyal supporter by addressing their concerns and demonstrating your willingness to listen. Tailor your responses to show empathy and understanding, while also providing solutions or explanations where applicable.

It's also beneficial to create a feedback loop by inviting your audience to share their thoughts and suggestions regularly. Encourage open communication by asking specific questions related to your content or brand. This proactive approach not only helps in mitigating negative feedback by addressing potential issues early on but also fosters a sense of community and involvement among your viewers.

Additionally, it's important to recognize that not all negative feedback is constructive. Trolls and malicious commenters can detract from productive discussions. In such cases, it's essential to have a clear strategy for moderating comments to maintain a positive and respectful environment on your channel. Utilize YouTube's moderation tools to filter out spam and abusive comments, allowing you to focus on genuine feedback that can help your brand grow.

Remember, your YouTube channel is a reflection of your brand's values and mission. By handling negative feedback with grace and professionalism, you reinforce your brand's integrity and build trust with your audience. This trust is invaluable, as it encourages viewers to engage more openly and honestly, ultimately leading to a more vibrant and interactive community.

In the ever-evolving landscape of digital media, the ability to effectively manage negative feedback is a vital skill. By embracing criticism as an opportunity for growth and maintaining a constructive dialogue with your audience, you not only enhance your content but also fortify the relationship with your viewers, ensuring the long-term success of your YouTube channel.

MAINTAINING ETHICAL STANDARDS

In the bustling digital landscape of YouTube, where millions of creators are vying for attention, it's easy to get caught up in the race for views, likes, and subscribers. However, as a brand, it's imperative to remember that maintaining ethical standards is not just a choice but a necessity. Ethical standards shape the perception of your brand, build trust with your audience, and ensure long-term success.

When setting up a YouTube channel for your brand, the first step in maintaining ethical standards is transparency. Be clear about your intentions, whether you're promoting a product, sharing knowledge, or entertaining. Disclose any affiliations, sponsorships, or partnerships to your audience. This transparency fosters trust and keeps your audience informed about potential biases. For instance, if you're reviewing a product, make it known if you've received it for free or if you're being compensated for the review. Honesty in your communications will resonate with your viewers and set you apart as a trustworthy brand.

Another critical aspect of ethical standards is respecting intellectual property. The temptation to use copyrighted material without permission can be strong, especially when it can enhance the appeal of your content. However, using music, images, or video clips without authorization can lead to legal issues and damage your brand's reputation. Instead, opt for royalty-free content or create original material. This not only keeps you on the right side of the law but also showcases your brand's creativity and commitment to ethical practices.

Moreover, consider the impact of your content on your audience and society at large. Avoid spreading misinformation or engaging in sensationalism for the sake of views. Misinformation can not only mislead your audience but also erode trust in your brand. Prioritize accuracy and integrity in your content. If your channel focuses on educational or informative content, ensure that your information is well-researched and fact-checked. Your audience will appreciate the effort and rely on your channel as a credible source of information.

In addition, be mindful of the comments and interactions on your channel. Foster a community that is respectful and inclusive. Monitor comments for inappropriate or harmful language and take action when necessary. Your audience should feel safe and valued when engaging with your brand. By promoting a positive and respectful community, you enhance your brand's reputation and create a loyal following.

Lastly, remember that your YouTube channel is an extension of your brand's identity. The values you communicate through your content should align with your brand's core principles. Whether it's commitment to sustainability, diversity, or innovation, ensure these values are reflected consistently across your channel. This consistency reinforces your brand's message and mission to your audience.

In the competitive arena of YouTube, adhering to ethical standards is not merely a guideline but a strategic advantage. By prioritizing transparency, respecting intellectual property, ensuring accuracy, fostering a positive community, and aligning with your brand's values, you not only safeguard your brand's reputation but also build a strong, trustworthy relationship with your audience. These ethical practices are the foundation of a successful and respected YouTube channel for your brand.

Chapter 10: Integrating YouTube with Other Marketing Channels

CROSS-PROMOTION WITH SOCIAL MEDIA

In today's digital age, leveraging the power of social media is not merely an option; it is a necessity for brands looking to thrive. By integrating your YouTube channel with various social media platforms, you can amplify your reach, enhance engagement, and ultimately drive more traffic to your content. Imagine your YouTube channel not as an isolated entity but as a vibrant part of a larger digital ecosystem. Each social media platform offers unique opportunities to connect with different segments of your audience, and by cross-promoting your YouTube content, you can ensure your message resonates far and wide.

Firstly, consider the sheer volume of active users on platforms like Instagram, Facebook, and Twitter. These platforms are bustling hubs of activity where your target audience is already spending a significant portion of their time. By sharing snippets, teasers, or behind-the-scenes content from your YouTube videos, you can pique the interest of potential viewers, enticing them to visit your channel for the full experience. Use eye-catching visuals and compelling captions to capture their attention and create a sense of anticipation.

Moreover, social media is an excellent arena for fostering community engagement. Platforms such as Instagram and Twitter allow for direct interaction with your audience through comments, likes, and shares. Use these interactions to build relationships and encourage dialogue around your YouTube content. Ask questions, respond to feedback, and create polls related to your videos to spark conversation and make your audience feel valued. This level of engagement not only drives traffic to your YouTube channel but also cultivates a loyal community around your brand.

Additionally, social media provides an unparalleled opportunity for targeted promotion. With advanced analytics and advertising options, you can tailor your promotional efforts to reach the right audience at the right time. Use these tools to promote your YouTube videos to users who have shown interest in similar content or who fit your ideal customer profile. By doing so, you increase the likelihood of attracting viewers who are genuinely interested in what you have to offer, leading to higher watch times and better engagement rates on your channel.

It's also crucial to maintain a consistent brand voice across all platforms. This consistency reinforces your brand identity and makes your content instantly recognizable, no matter where your audience encounters it. Develop a cohesive strategy that aligns your YouTube content with your broader social media presence. This might involve using similar graphics, color schemes, or messaging across all platforms to create a unified brand image.

Finally, don't underestimate the power of collaboration. Partnering with influencers or brands that align with your values can expand your reach exponentially. Collaborations allow you to tap into new audiences who may not have discovered your YouTube channel otherwise. By cross-promoting content, you not only gain exposure to a wider audience but also enhance your credibility and authority in your niche.

Utilizing social media for cross-promotion is a dynamic and effective way to grow your YouTube channel. By reaching out to your audience where they already are, engaging with them on a personal level, and maintaining a consistent brand image, you can create a thriving online presence that drives your brand forward.

INCORPORATING YOUTUBE INTO EMAIL MARKETING

Email marketing remains one of the most powerful tools for brands to connect with their audience, but integrating YouTube into this strategy can elevate your campaigns to new heights. By combining the visual appeal of video content with the direct reach of email, brands can create dynamic, engaging experiences that drive higher engagement rates and foster deeper connections with subscribers. This approach not only enhances the value of your email communications but also maximizes the impact of your YouTube content.

Imagine sending out an email that not only informs but also captivates. Including YouTube videos in your emails does exactly that. Videos are inherently more engaging than text alone, capturing attention in a way that static content cannot. By embedding or linking to your YouTube videos, you can provide subscribers with a richer, more interactive experience. This is particularly effective when showcasing product demonstrations, customer testimonials, or behind-the-scenes content that tells your brand's story in a compelling way.

Furthermore, incorporating YouTube into your email marketing strategy can significantly increase your channel's visibility and subscriber count. Each email you send becomes an opportunity to promote your YouTube channel to a potentially vast audience. Encourage your subscribers to watch, like, and share your videos, and invite them to subscribe to your channel for regular updates. This cross-promotion can lead to exponential growth in your YouTube audience as your email subscribers become your channel subscribers.

Using email to drive traffic to your YouTube channel also allows for greater targeting and personalization. By segmenting your email list, you can tailor your video content to the specific interests and behaviors of different subscriber groups. For example, you might send product tutorial videos to customers who have recently made a purchase or share industry insights with subscribers who have shown interest in thought leadership content. This level of personalization can increase the likelihood that recipients will engage with your videos and take the desired action, whether that's subscribing to your channel, visiting your website, or making a purchase.

Moreover, video content can enhance the storytelling aspect of your brand's emails. It allows you to convey emotions and narratives that resonate with your audience on a deeper level. Whether you're launching a new product, sharing a customer success story, or providing educational content, videos can make your message more memorable and impactful. This not only helps in retaining customer interest but also in building a loyal community around your brand.

To effectively incorporate YouTube into your email marketing, ensure that your emails are optimized for mobile devices, as a significant portion of email opens occur on smartphones and tablets. Additionally, use clear, compelling calls to action that encourage viewers to watch your videos and engage with your content. By strategically integrating YouTube into your email marketing efforts, you can create a seamless and powerful communication channel that leverages the strengths of both platforms, ultimately driving growth and success for your brand.

UTILIZING INFLUENCER PARTNERSHIPS

In today's digital landscape, influencer partnerships are not just an option; they are a necessity for brands aiming to establish a strong presence on YouTube. Leveraging the power of influencers can significantly amplify your brand's reach, enhance credibility, and foster a deeper connection with your target audience. These partnerships offer a strategic avenue to tap into established communities, allowing your brand to be seen and heard by thousands, if not millions, of potential customers.

The first step in harnessing the power of influencer collaborations is identifying the right influencers who align with your brand values and audience interests. It's crucial to conduct thorough research to find influencers whose content, style, and audience demographics match your brand's persona. This alignment ensures that the partnership feels authentic and resonates well with both the influencer's followers and your potential customers.

Once you've identified potential influencers, reach out with a personalized proposal that clearly outlines the mutual benefits of collaborating. Influencers are more likely to engage when they see genuine interest and value in the partnership. Highlight how this collaboration will enhance their content, offer exclusive opportunities, or provide unique experiences for their audience. By positioning the partnership as a win-win scenario, you increase the likelihood of securing enthusiastic and committed collaborators.

After establishing a partnership, it's important to collaborate closely with the influencer to create content that seamlessly integrates your brand while maintaining their authentic voice. Influencers have built their audience based on trust and authenticity, and any perceived inauthenticity can be detrimental to both parties. Therefore, work together to brainstorm creative ideas that align with both your brand's objectives and the influencer's content style. Whether it's a product review, a tutorial, or a behind-the-scenes look at your brand, the content should feel natural and engaging.

Furthermore, consider offering influencers creative freedom to experiment with content formats that they know will resonate with their audience. This level of trust can lead to innovative and impactful content that might exceed your expectations. Remember, influencers understand their audience better than anyone else, and their insights can be invaluable in crafting messages that strike a chord with viewers.

Additionally, measure the success of your influencer partnerships by tracking key performance indicators such as engagement rates, audience reach, and conversion metrics. Analyzing this data will provide insights into what works and what doesn't, allowing you to refine your approach for future collaborations. It's essential to maintain open communication with influencers throughout the partnership to gather feedback and make necessary adjustments to maximize results.

By strategically utilizing influencer partnerships, you can create a powerful synergy that elevates your brand's presence on YouTube. These collaborations can drive brand awareness, foster authentic connections, and ultimately contribute to your brand's growth. As you venture into this dynamic realm, remember that the key to successful influencer partnerships lies in finding the right match, fostering authentic relationships, and continuously adapting your strategies to meet the evolving needs of your audience.

LEVERAGING YOUTUBE FOR PR

In the dynamic landscape of digital communication, YouTube stands as a powerhouse platform that transcends traditional boundaries, offering brands an unprecedented opportunity to amplify their public relations efforts. By harnessing the visual and interactive nature of YouTube, brands can craft compelling narratives that engage audiences on a global scale, fostering deeper connections and enhancing brand reputation.

YouTube's vast reach and diverse user base make it an ideal platform for PR activities. Unlike traditional media, where messages are often filtered through intermediaries, YouTube allows brands to communicate directly with their audience. This direct line of communication enables brands to present their stories authentically and transparently, fostering trust and credibility. By creating content that resonates with their target audience, brands can position themselves as thought leaders and influencers within their industry.

Moreover, YouTube's algorithm favors engaging content, which means that well-crafted videos have the potential to reach viral status, exponentially increasing a brand's visibility. This organic reach is invaluable for PR campaigns, as it allows brands to reach new audiences without significant advertising spend. Furthermore, YouTube's analytics tools provide detailed insights into audience demographics and engagement, enabling brands to refine their PR strategies and tailor content to meet the preferences and interests of their viewers.

Another significant advantage of utilizing YouTube for PR is the platform's ability to humanize a brand. Through behind-the-scenes footage, interviews, and storytelling, brands can showcase their values, culture, and the people behind the products. This personal touch not only enhances relatability but also strengthens emotional connections with the audience. In an era where consumers increasingly seek authenticity and transparency, this human element can be a powerful differentiator.

Collaborations with influencers and content creators on YouTube further extend a brand's reach and credibility. By partnering with individuals who align with their brand values, companies can tap into new audiences and leverage the trust and loyalty that these influencers have cultivated with their followers. These collaborations can take various forms, from product reviews and tutorials to co-created content that integrates the brand message seamlessly.

Live streaming on YouTube offers another dimension of engagement, allowing brands to interact with their audience in real-time. Whether it's a product launch, Q&A session, or virtual event, live streaming creates a sense of immediacy and exclusivity that can enhance PR initiatives. It provides an opportunity to address questions and feedback directly, demonstrating responsiveness and commitment to customer satisfaction.

Incorporating YouTube into a brand's PR strategy is not just about creating content; it's about crafting a cohesive narrative that aligns with the brand's overall messaging and goals. Consistency in messaging, tone, and visual identity across all videos strengthens brand recognition and reinforces the brand's position in the market.

By leveraging YouTube's capabilities for PR, brands can not only reach wider audiences but also build lasting relationships with their viewers. In a digital age where attention is a valuable currency, YouTube offers a platform where brands can not only capture but also hold the attention of their audience, driving engagement and fostering brand loyalty.

Chapter 11: Scaling Your YouTube Channel

INVESTING IN ADVANCED EQUIPMENT

In an era where digital presence can make or break a brand, setting up a YouTube channel stands as one of the most potent strategies to amplify your brand's voice. Yet, while content is king, the quality of your presentation can often determine whether your audience stays engaged or clicks away. Investing in advanced equipment for your YouTube channel is not merely a recommendation; it is a necessity for anyone serious about building a credible and influential online presence.

Imagine watching a video where the sound crackles, the image is grainy, and the lighting is poor. No matter how valuable the information, the likelihood of viewers losing interest is high. High-quality equipment transforms your channel from amateurish to professional, aligning your brand with excellence and reliability. Viewers equate quality production with trustworthiness, and this trust can translate into greater viewer retention, subscriber growth, and ultimately, brand loyalty.

The visual and auditory impact of your videos is your first impression, and in the fast-paced world of digital media, first impressions are everything. Investing in a good quality camera ensures that your videos are crisp and clear, capturing the essence of your content with precision. A high-quality microphone is equally critical, as clear audio is often more important than visual quality; audiences are more forgiving of subpar visuals than they are of poor sound. Lighting, too, plays a crucial role in setting the tone and mood of your content, highlighting your subject and making your videos aesthetically pleasing.

Moreover, advanced equipment opens doors to creative possibilities that basic tools simply cannot offer. With professional-grade cameras, you can experiment with different shooting techniques and angles, enhancing the storytelling aspect of your videos. Superior microphones allow you to capture a wider range of sounds, adding depth and richness to your audio. Quality lighting lets you play with shadows and highlights, creating visually striking content that stands out in a crowded digital landscape.

Investing in advanced equipment is also an investment in your brand's future. As your channel grows, so too will the expectations of your audience. Having the right equipment from the start means you are prepared to meet these expectations and produce content that evolves with your brand. It also positions you to take advantage of new trends and technologies, keeping your content fresh and relevant.

While the initial cost of advanced equipment might seem daunting, consider it a long-term investment. The return on this investment comes in the form of increased viewer engagement, higher subscription rates, and enhanced brand perception. Moreover, high-quality equipment often has a longer lifespan, providing value over time and reducing the need for frequent upgrades.

In choosing to invest in advanced equipment, you are not just buying tools; you are buying the potential for your brand's success on YouTube. It is a strategic decision that signals your commitment to quality and your dedication to providing your audience with the best possible experience. Make the investment, and watch as your channel transforms into a powerful platform for your brand's message.

EXPANDING YOUR TEAM

As your YouTube channel begins to gain traction, the demands of content creation, marketing, and community engagement can quickly become overwhelming. Expanding your team is not just a luxury but a necessity to sustain growth and maintain the quality of your brand's presence. A well-rounded team can bring fresh perspectives, diverse skills, and increased efficiency, allowing you to focus on strategic decisions and creative vision.

Finding the right people starts with identifying the roles that will most benefit your channel. Consider hiring a content strategist who can help plan your video calendar, ensuring a consistent and engaging output that resonates with your audience. This role is crucial for aligning your content with your brand's goals and for keeping up with the latest trends and audience preferences.

Next, think about bringing on board a talented video editor. While you might have started editing your own videos, a professional editor can elevate your content with polished visuals, seamless transitions, and creative effects that captivate viewers. This frees up your time to focus on content creation and other strategic aspects of growing your channel.

Another vital role is a social media manager. This person will be responsible for promoting your videos across various platforms, engaging with your audience, and building a community around your brand. A good social media manager can increase your channel's visibility and drive traffic by crafting compelling posts and interacting with viewers in a way that aligns with your brand's voice and values.

Consider the benefits of collaborating with a graphic designer as well. Eye-catching thumbnails, channel banners, and other visual elements are essential for attracting viewers and making a strong first impression. A designer can help create a cohesive visual identity that sets your channel apart from competitors and reinforces your brand's message.

Moreover, hiring a marketing specialist can significantly impact your channel's growth. This expert can devise strategies to increase your subscriber count, boost video views, and improve overall engagement. By analyzing data and understanding viewer behavior, a marketing specialist can refine your approach to reach a wider audience effectively.

Don't overlook the importance of a community manager, especially as your channel grows. This role focuses on fostering a positive and active community by responding to comments, moderating discussions, and gathering feedback. A community manager helps create a sense of belonging among your viewers, turning casual viewers into loyal fans.

As you expand your team, emphasize the importance of collaboration and communication. Encourage open dialogue and regular meetings to ensure everyone is aligned with your channel's objectives and brand ethos. This collaborative environment fosters creativity and innovation, driving your channel's success.

In conclusion, building a team is a strategic investment in your channel's future. By bringing in skilled professionals, you not only enhance the quality of your content but also free yourself to focus on what you do best: creating and connecting with your audience. As your team grows, so will your channel, establishing your brand as a formidable presence on YouTube.

EXPLORING INTERNATIONAL MARKETS

In today's digital age, the world is more interconnected than ever, providing brands with unprecedented opportunities to reach global audiences. Setting up a YouTube channel for your brand is not just about broadcasting to your local market; it's about tapping into a vast international audience hungry for content that resonates with them. Expanding into international markets through YouTube can be a game-changer for your brand, offering numerous benefits that can elevate your business to new heights.

Firstly, consider the sheer volume of potential viewers. YouTube boasts over 2 billion logged-in monthly users, with a significant portion residing outside of your home country. By creating content that appeals to international audiences, your brand can engage with millions of potential customers who are eager to discover new and exciting products or services. The key is to understand the cultural nuances and preferences of these diverse viewers, tailoring your content to meet their unique needs and interests.

One effective strategy is to conduct thorough market research to identify which countries or regions have a high demand for your brand's offerings. By understanding the specific trends and consumer behaviors in these markets, you can create content that is not only relevant but also compelling. This might involve translating your videos into different languages, using culturally appropriate imagery, or collaborating with local influencers who already have a strong presence in those markets. Such efforts can significantly enhance your brand's credibility and relatability, making it easier for international audiences to connect with your content.

Moreover, leveraging YouTube's advanced analytics tools can provide valuable insights into how your content is performing in different regions. By analyzing metrics such as watch time, engagement rates, and audience demographics, you can fine-tune your strategy to optimize your reach and impact in each market. This data-driven approach ensures that your efforts are focused on the areas with the highest potential return on investment.

Additionally, expanding into international markets via YouTube can lead to increased brand recognition and trust. As your channel gains traction across different regions, your brand becomes more familiar to potential customers, building a sense of trust and authority. This can lead to higher conversion rates, as viewers are more likely to purchase from a brand they recognize and trust.

Furthermore, reaching international audiences can foster innovation within your brand. Exposure to different cultures and consumer preferences can inspire new ideas and approaches, driving product development and marketing strategies that are fresh and exciting. This not only keeps your brand relevant but also positions it as a leader in the global market.

Incorporating a global perspective into your YouTube strategy is not just an option; it is a necessity for brands looking to thrive in the digital era. By exploring international markets and crafting content that resonates with diverse audiences, your brand can unlock new growth opportunities, establish a strong global presence, and ultimately achieve long-term success on YouTube.

PLANNING FOR LONG-TERM GROWTH

Creating a YouTube channel for your brand is a pivotal step in expanding your digital presence, but the real magic lies in planning for long-term growth. This is not just about gaining a handful of subscribers or a few viral videos; it's about establishing a sustainable strategy that will continually attract and engage your audience. Your channel should be viewed as a dynamic ecosystem that evolves with your brand and consistently delivers value to your viewers.

The first step in planning for long-term growth is understanding your audience. This requires deep insights into their preferences, behaviors, and needs. Utilize YouTube Analytics to monitor which types of content resonate most with your viewers. Pay attention to metrics like watch time, audience retention, and demographics. This data is invaluable in shaping your content strategy, ensuring that your videos align with what your audience is seeking.

Consistency is another cornerstone of long-term growth. Establish a regular posting schedule that your audience can rely on. This not only helps in retaining your current subscribers but also attracts new ones. Consistency builds trust, and trust is a vital component of any brand's success. However, consistency doesn't mean sacrificing quality. Each video should be crafted with care, offering something unique and worthwhile to your audience.

Diversifying your content is also crucial. While it's important to have a niche, exploring different types of content can attract a broader audience. Consider incorporating tutorials, behind-the-scenes looks, interviews, or live streams. Each format provides a different way to engage with your audience and keeps your channel fresh and exciting.

Collaborations can significantly boost your channel's growth. Partnering with other YouTubers or brands in your niche can introduce your channel to new audiences. It's a mutually beneficial strategy that can lead to increased exposure and credibility. When choosing collaborators, ensure their values align with your brand to maintain authenticity.

SEO optimization should never be overlooked. Use relevant keywords in your video titles, descriptions, and tags to improve discoverability. An optimized channel is more likely to appear in search results, increasing the chances of attracting new viewers. Additionally, creating compelling thumbnails and engaging titles can entice potential subscribers to click on your videos.

Building a community around your channel is essential for sustainable growth. Engage with your audience through comments, respond to their feedback, and encourage discussions. This interaction fosters a sense of belonging among your viewers and can turn casual viewers into loyal subscribers. Consider creating a dedicated space for your community, such as a Facebook group or Discord server, where fans can interact with you and each other.

Finally, remain adaptable. The digital landscape is ever-changing, and so are audience preferences. Stay informed about the latest trends and be willing to adjust your strategy accordingly. Experiment with new ideas and be open to feedback. This flexibility will not only help your channel grow but also keep it relevant in a competitive environment.

By implementing these strategies, you can ensure that your YouTube channel is not just a fleeting presence but a thriving platform that supports your brand's long-term growth.

Chapter 12: Case Studies and Success Stories

BRANDS THAT THRIVED ON YOUTUBE

In the ever-evolving landscape of digital marketing, YouTube stands out as a formidable platform that has propelled numerous brands to unprecedented success. Its power lies not just in its vast audience but in the unique ability to engage viewers with compelling visual narratives. Brands that have thrived on YouTube have harnessed this potential, transforming their identities and expanding their reach in ways that traditional media could never achieve.

Consider the meteoric rise of Dollar Shave Club. When they launched their now-famous video, 'Our Blades Are F***ing Great,' it was a strategic masterstroke that blended humor with direct engagement. This video not only went viral but also positioned Dollar Shave Club as a disruptive force in the shaving industry. By creating content that resonated with their target audience, they turned viewers into loyal customers, proving that a well-crafted YouTube strategy can redefine a brand's trajectory.

Similarly, the beauty industry has seen remarkable success stories, with brands like Glossier effectively utilizing YouTube to build a community around their products. By leveraging tutorials, testimonials, and influencer partnerships, Glossier has cultivated an authentic brand image that resonates with their audience. They've created a sense of belonging among their customers, who feel they are part of a larger conversation about beauty and self-expression. This sense of community is a powerful driver of brand loyalty and advocacy.

Another standout example is Red Bull, a brand synonymous with extreme sports and high-octane adventures. Red Bull has harnessed YouTube's platform to create a vast array of content that extends far beyond traditional advertising. Their channel features everything from high-energy sports events to documentaries that capture the spirit of adventure. By aligning their brand with thrilling experiences, Red Bull has effectively communicated their brand ethos, attracting millions of subscribers and solidifying their position as a leader in lifestyle branding.

Beyond these examples, countless other brands have thrived on YouTube by understanding the platform's unique dynamics. They recognize that success on YouTube requires more than just high-quality content; it demands a deep understanding of audience engagement and the ability to tell stories that resonate on a personal level. These brands have developed strategies that prioritize authenticity, creativity, and community-building, ensuring that their content not only reaches viewers but also leaves a lasting impact.

The common thread among these successful brands is their commitment to creating content that is not only entertaining but also adds value to the viewer's experience. They understand that YouTube is not just a platform for advertising but a space for building relationships and fostering a sense of connection with their audience. By focusing on authenticity and engagement, these brands have not only thrived on YouTube but have set new standards for what it means to succeed in the digital age. For any brand looking to make its mark, the lessons from these trailblazers are invaluable, offering a roadmap to harnessing YouTube's potential and achieving remarkable growth.

LEARNING FROM YOUTUBE FAILURES

Navigating the world of YouTube can be daunting, but recognizing and analyzing the failures of others can provide invaluable lessons in crafting a successful channel for your brand. Many content creators have ventured onto this platform with high hopes, only to falter due to common pitfalls that can be avoided with careful planning and strategy. Understanding these mistakes can save you time, resources, and frustration, allowing you to build a channel that truly resonates with your audience.

One of the most prevalent mistakes is the lack of a clear niche or focus. Some creators attempt to cover an array of unrelated topics, hoping to capture a broad audience. However, this approach often results in a diluted brand message that fails to engage viewers. Instead, focus on a specific niche that aligns with your brand values and expertise. This targeted approach not only helps in building a loyal subscriber base but also positions your channel as a go-to resource for specific content, enhancing your brand's credibility.

Another common error is neglecting the importance of consistency. Posting sporadically or with irregular quality can quickly disengage your audience. Establishing a consistent upload schedule and maintaining a standard for content quality are crucial for retaining viewer interest. This consistency builds trust and anticipation among your audience, encouraging them to return for more. Planning your content calendar and adhering to it diligently can significantly improve your channel's performance.

Equally important is understanding the role of audience interaction. Many creators overlook the power of engaging with their audience through comments, social media, and other platforms. Ignoring viewer feedback or failing to foster a sense of community can alienate your audience. Actively responding to comments, acknowledging viewer suggestions, and creating content that reflects audience interests can strengthen the connection between your brand and its followers, fostering loyalty and encouraging word-of-mouth promotion.

Moreover, the significance of optimizing video titles, descriptions, and thumbnails cannot be overstated. These elements are the first touchpoints for potential viewers and play a critical role in attracting clicks. Ignoring SEO best practices or creating unappealing thumbnails can severely limit your channel's reach. Crafting engaging titles, using relevant keywords, and designing eye-catching thumbnails are essential strategies for maximizing visibility and drawing in viewers.

Lastly, many YouTube channels falter due to a lack of adaptability. The digital landscape is ever-evolving, and staying attuned to changes in platform algorithms, viewer preferences, and industry trends is vital. Rigid adherence to outdated strategies can lead to stagnation. Instead, remain flexible and willing to experiment with new content formats, styles, or technologies to keep your channel fresh and relevant.

By learning from these common failures, you can establish a robust foundation for your YouTube channel. This proactive approach not only helps in avoiding potential setbacks but also positions your brand as a dynamic and engaging presence in the digital realm. With careful strategy and execution, your YouTube channel can become a powerful tool for brand growth and audience engagement.

INNOVATIVE CONTENT STRATEGIES

In the ever-evolving landscape of digital media, establishing a YouTube channel that stands out requires more than just regular uploads. It demands a strategic approach to content creation that resonates with your target audience and amplifies your brand's voice. Innovative content strategies are the cornerstone of a successful YouTube presence, enabling brands to capture attention, foster engagement, and build a loyal community of followers.

To begin with, understanding your audience is paramount. Dive deep into analytics to uncover what content appeals most to your viewers. Are they drawn to tutorials, behind-the-scenes looks, or perhaps thought leadership pieces? Tailoring your content to meet these preferences not only increases viewer retention but also enhances the likelihood of your videos being shared across platforms, broadening your reach.

Incorporating storytelling into your videos can transform ordinary content into captivating narratives. Storytelling humanizes your brand, making it relatable and memorable. Craft stories that reflect your brand values, mission, and the unique benefits your products or services offer. This approach not only educates your audience but also evokes emotional connections, fostering stronger brand loyalty.

Another innovative strategy is to leverage collaborations. Partnering with influencers or complementary brands can introduce your channel to new audiences and add fresh perspectives to your content. When choosing collaborators, ensure their values and audience align with yours to maintain brand consistency and authenticity. These partnerships can take the form of co-hosted videos, guest appearances, or joint campaigns that serve mutual interests.

Interactive content is also a game-changer. Engaging with your audience through live streams, Q&A sessions, or polls invites viewers to participate actively, creating a sense of community. This interaction not only boosts viewer engagement but also provides valuable feedback and insights into your audience's preferences and expectations.

Moreover, diversifying your content formats can enhance your channel's appeal. Experiment with a mix of short and long-form videos, animations, vlogs, and interviews to keep your content fresh and dynamic. Each format offers unique advantages; for example, short videos are perfect for quick, impactful messages, while longer videos provide depth and detailed exploration of topics.

Investing in high-quality production can significantly elevate your content. While authenticity is crucial, well-produced videos with clear audio, sharp visuals, and professional editing convey a sense of credibility and professionalism. This doesn't necessarily mean breaking the bank – even small improvements in lighting, sound, and editing can make a noticeable difference.

Finally, staying abreast of trends and platform updates is vital. YouTube frequently updates its algorithms and features, and being early adopters of new tools can give your channel a competitive edge. Whether it's experimenting with YouTube Shorts, embracing 360-degree videos, or utilizing end screens and cards effectively, staying informed and adaptable can drive your channel's growth.

Incorporating these innovative strategies into your YouTube content plan can transform your channel from a simple brand extension into a vibrant, engaging platform that draws viewers in and keeps them coming back for more. Each strategy, when executed thoughtfully, builds towards a cohesive and compelling brand narrative that resonates in the digital space.

ADAPTATION AND RESILIENCE

In the ever-evolving landscape of digital content, setting up a YouTube channel for your brand demands more than just technical know-how; it requires the ability to adapt and the resilience to thrive amidst constant change. The digital world moves at a breakneck pace, with trends, algorithms, and viewer preferences shifting like the sands of time. To ensure your brand's success on YouTube, cultivating a mindset of adaptation and resilience is not just beneficial but essential.

Adaptation begins with a keen awareness of the platform's dynamics. YouTube is not static; its algorithms are constantly updated to enhance user experience. To stay relevant, you must remain informed about these changes and be willing to adjust your strategy accordingly. This might mean altering your content style, posting frequency, or even the platform features you utilize. For instance, if YouTube introduces a new feature like Shorts or Community posts, consider how these tools can be integrated into your content strategy to engage your audience more effectively.

Moreover, understanding your audience's evolving preferences is crucial. Regularly analyze your channel's analytics to gain insights into what content resonates most with your viewers. This data is invaluable for refining your content strategy and ensuring that you are meeting the needs and interests of your audience. Flexibility in content creation allows you to experiment with different formats and topics, keeping your channel fresh and engaging.

Resilience, on the other hand, is about maintaining your commitment and enthusiasm even when faced with setbacks. Building a successful YouTube channel is rarely a linear journey; it's filled with highs and lows. There will be times when videos do not perform as expected or when subscriber growth stagnates. During such times, resilience is your greatest ally. Instead of viewing these challenges as insurmountable obstacles, see them as opportunities for growth and learning. Every setback provides a chance to analyze what went wrong, recalibrate your approach, and emerge stronger.

Furthermore, resilience involves a long-term vision for your brand. Success on YouTube is often the result of consistent effort over time. It requires patience and perseverance, knowing that while viral success is possible, sustainable growth is achieved through dedication and continuous improvement. By focusing on your brand's core values and mission, you can remain steadfast in your objectives, regardless of temporary setbacks.

Incorporating adaptation and resilience into your YouTube strategy not only enhances your brand's potential for success but also enriches your creative process. Embrace change as a constant companion and view challenges as stepping stones to greater achievements. By doing so, you position your brand not just to survive, but to thrive in the dynamic world of digital content creation. Your ability to adapt and your resilience in the face of adversity will set your brand apart and ensure that your YouTube channel remains a powerful tool for engagement and growth.

Chapter 13: Future of YouTube and Conclusion

EMERGING TRENDS ON YOUTUBE

In the dynamic landscape of digital marketing, YouTube stands as a beacon of opportunity for brands seeking to expand their reach and engage with audiences in a meaningful way. The platform is not just a repository of videos; it is a thriving ecosystem where trends emerge and evolve, shaping the way brands connect with their consumers. As you contemplate setting up a YouTube channel for your brand, understanding these emerging trends is crucial to crafting a strategy that resonates and captivates.

The first trend that demands attention is the rise of short-form content. With the advent of YouTube Shorts, the platform has embraced the global shift towards bite-sized videos that capture attention quickly. This format is particularly appealing to younger audiences who crave fast-paced, engaging content. Brands that master the art of delivering impactful messages in under 60 seconds can leverage this trend to boost visibility and engagement.

Another significant trend is the increasing importance of authenticity and relatability. Today's viewers are drawn to content that feels genuine and personal. Brands that succeed on YouTube often do so by showcasing a human side, whether through behind-the-scenes glimpses, storytelling, or user-generated content. This trend underscores the necessity for brands to foster a community around their channel, encouraging interaction and dialogue with their audience.

Live streaming is also gaining momentum as a powerful tool for real-time engagement. The immediacy and interactivity of live streams allow brands to connect with their audience on a more personal level. Whether it's a product launch, a Q&A session, or a live tutorial, this format provides a unique opportunity to engage viewers directly and foster a sense of community.

Moreover, the integration of shoppable videos is transforming YouTube into a more commerce-friendly platform. This trend enables brands to seamlessly blend content and commerce, offering viewers the ability to purchase products directly from videos. For brands, this means turning engagement into tangible sales, making YouTube a pivotal part of an omnichannel marketing strategy.

The focus on diversity and inclusion is another critical trend shaping content on YouTube. As audiences demand more representation, brands are called to reflect this in their content. By showcasing diverse voices and perspectives, brands can not only broaden their appeal but also demonstrate their commitment to social values, fostering deeper connections with their audience.

Finally, the rise of educational content highlights YouTube's role as a learning hub. Brands that provide value through informative and educational videos can position themselves as thought leaders in their industry. This trend is particularly beneficial for brands in niches where expertise and knowledge are highly valued.

Harnessing these trends requires a proactive approach and a willingness to adapt to the ever-changing digital landscape. For brands, the key to success on YouTube lies in staying informed, being agile, and most importantly, creating content that not only aligns with these trends but also resonates with their target audience. By doing so, a brand can establish a compelling presence on YouTube, turning viewers into loyal supporters and advocates.

PREPARING FOR TECHNOLOGICAL ADVANCEMENTS

In the rapidly evolving digital landscape, staying ahead of technological advancements is not just a luxury but a necessity for anyone looking to establish a successful YouTube channel for their brand. The pace at which technology transforms can be overwhelming, yet it offers unprecedented opportunities to enhance your content, reach wider audiences, and streamline your workflow. Harnessing these advancements effectively can set your brand apart in a crowded marketplace.

First, consider the tools and equipment that can elevate your video production quality. Investing in high-definition cameras, professional lighting, and quality microphones can significantly enhance the visual and auditory experience for your viewers. As technology progresses, these tools become more accessible and affordable, allowing even small brands to produce content that rivals that of larger competitors. Staying informed about the latest equipment trends ensures that your channel maintains a professional edge.

Moreover, software advancements in video editing and graphics can dramatically improve the aesthetics of your content. Utilizing state-of-the-art editing software allows for seamless transitions, dynamic effects, and polished final products. Familiarizing yourself with tools such as Adobe Premiere Pro, Final Cut Pro, or even more user-friendly options like iMovie or Canva can make a substantial difference in the quality of your uploads. Regularly updating your skillset with the latest features and techniques in these programs can keep your content fresh and engaging.

Artificial Intelligence (AI) and machine learning are revolutionizing content creation and audience interaction. AI-driven analytics tools can provide deep insights into viewer behavior, helping you tailor your content to meet the preferences and interests of your audience. Understanding these analytics allows you to refine your content strategy, ensuring that your videos not only reach but resonate with your target market. Additionally, AI can assist in automating tasks such as video editing, captioning, and even content curation, freeing up valuable time for creative development.

Virtual reality (VR) and augmented reality (AR) are also becoming integral to digital storytelling. Incorporating VR and AR elements into your videos can provide immersive experiences that captivate audiences and encourage greater engagement. While these technologies are still emerging, early adoption can position your brand as an innovator and leader in your industry.

Furthermore, staying abreast of platform-specific technological updates is crucial. YouTube frequently updates its algorithms, monetization policies, and features. Understanding these changes and adapting your channel strategy accordingly can optimize your channel's visibility and profitability. Engaging with YouTube's Creator Academy and community forums can provide valuable insights and tips directly from the platform.

In an era where technology shapes consumer expectations, preparing for and adapting to these technological advancements is vital for the longevity and success of your YouTube channel. By embracing new tools, software, and trends, you not only enhance your content but also build a brand that is forward-thinking and responsive to change. This proactive approach not only attracts viewers but also establishes a loyal community that grows alongside your brand's digital journey.

SUSTAINING YOUR CHANNEL'S RELEVANCE

In the rapidly evolving world of digital content, maintaining the relevance of your YouTube channel is not just advantageous—it's essential for the survival and growth of your brand. The digital landscape is saturated with countless channels vying for viewers' attention, making it crucial to consistently innovate and adapt to sustain your channel's relevance. To achieve this, a strategic approach is necessary, encompassing the understanding of viewer needs, leveraging analytics, and embracing technological advancements.

First, understanding your audience is paramount. Your channel must align with the interests and preferences of your viewers, which are continually evolving. Regularly engage with your audience through comments, polls, and community posts to gather insights into what they value most. This direct feedback loop enables you to tailor your content to meet their expectations, ensuring that your channel remains a go-to source for your particular niche. By creating content that resonates with your audience, you not only retain existing viewers but also attract new ones.

Moreover, leveraging analytics is a powerful tool in maintaining your channel's relevance. YouTube provides a wealth of data regarding viewer demographics, watch time, and engagement rates. By analyzing these metrics, you can identify trends and patterns that inform your content strategy. Pay attention to which videos perform well and why, then replicate and expand upon these successes. Additionally, monitor the performance of different video formats and topics to diversify your content offerings effectively. The key is to remain flexible and responsive to the data, allowing it to guide your creative decisions.

Another critical aspect is staying updated with technological advancements. YouTube frequently updates its platform with new features and tools that can enhance your channel's reach and engagement. Whether it's utilizing YouTube Shorts to capture the attention of a broader audience or experimenting with live streaming to create real-time interactions, embracing these innovations can set your channel apart from the competition. Furthermore, incorporating high-quality production techniques, such as using better equipment or software, can significantly impact the viewer's experience, keeping your content fresh and engaging.

Collaborations and networking also play a vital role in sustaining relevance. Partnering with other creators or influencers can introduce your channel to new audiences and provide fresh perspectives on content creation. These collaborations can take various forms, from guest appearances to joint projects, and often result in mutual growth and increased visibility.

Lastly, consider the broader context of your brand and its positioning within the market. Stay informed about industry trends and shifts in consumer behavior, and be prepared to pivot your content strategy accordingly. By aligning your channel with the evolving landscape of your industry, you ensure that it remains pertinent and valuable to your audience.

In a world where digital content is continuously consumed at an unprecedented rate, sustaining your YouTube channel's relevance is a dynamic and ongoing process. By understanding your audience, leveraging analytics, embracing technological advancements, fostering collaborations, and staying attuned to market trends, you can ensure that your channel not only survives but thrives in the competitive digital arena.

FINAL THOUGHTS AND ENCOURAGEMENT

Launching a YouTube channel for your brand is a strategic move that holds immense potential for growth and engagement. The digital landscape is vast and ever-evolving, but with the right approach, your brand can secure its place and thrive. This endeavor is not just about creating content; it's about crafting a compelling narrative that resonates with your audience and aligns with your brand's values.

As you set up your channel, remember that consistency is key. Regular uploads not only keep your audience engaged but also signal to YouTube's algorithms that your channel is active and worth promoting. Develop a content calendar that aligns with your brand's goals and stick to it. This disciplined approach will build anticipation and loyalty among your viewers.

Quality should never be compromised for quantity. Invest in good equipment and editing software to ensure your videos are professional and polished. However, authenticity is equally important. Your audience connects with genuine content that reflects your brand's personality. Strive for a balance between professionalism and authenticity to build trust and rapport with your viewers.

Engagement is the lifeblood of a successful YouTube channel. Encourage your audience to comment, share, and subscribe. Respond to their comments and feedback, fostering a community around your brand. This interaction not only boosts your channel's visibility but also provides valuable insights into your audience's preferences and interests.

Promotion is another crucial aspect of your channel's growth. Leverage your existing social media platforms to drive traffic to your YouTube channel. Collaborate with influencers or other brands to reach a wider audience. These strategies can significantly increase your channel's exposure and subscriber base.

Analytics should be your guiding light as you navigate the world of YouTube. Regularly review your channel's performance metrics to understand what works and what doesn't. This data-driven approach will help you refine your content strategy and maximize your channel's potential.

The journey of establishing a YouTube channel for your brand is filled with challenges and opportunities. Stay committed to your vision and remain adaptable to the changing trends and audience behaviors. Your persistence and dedication will pay off as you watch your brand's presence grow in the digital realm.

Remember, success doesn't happen overnight. It requires patience, creativity, and a willingness to learn from both successes and setbacks. Keep pushing forward, and let your passion for your brand guide you. With time, effort, and strategic planning, your YouTube channel can become a powerful tool in your brand's marketing arsenal.

Believe in the power of your content to inspire, educate, and entertain your audience. Your brand's story is unique, and YouTube offers a platform to share it with the world. Let this be the beginning of a rewarding journey that elevates your brand and connects you with a global audience.

EPILOGUE

As you reach the end of this guide, you now possess the knowledge and tools to establish a successful YouTube channel for your brand. The digital landscape is ever-evolving, and staying informed about the latest trends and technologies will be crucial for your continued growth. The strategies and insights shared in this book are designed to help you navigate the complexities of YouTube in 2025, from content creation to audience engagement and beyond.

Reflect on the importance of authenticity and connection in your content. The power of storytelling remains one of the most effective ways to engage viewers and build a loyal community. Your unique brand voice and perspective are what will set you apart in a crowded digital space. Remember, consistency is key. Regularly uploading content and interacting with your audience can significantly boost your channel's visibility and subscriber count.

Consider the value of collaboration and networking with other creators. Building relationships within the YouTube community can open doors to new opportunities and provide valuable insights into different content strategies and audience engagement techniques. Additionally, keep an eye on analytics to understand your audience's preferences and adapt your content accordingly.

As you continue to grow your channel, don't shy away from experimenting with new formats and ideas. The YouTube platform offers endless possibilities for creativity and innovation. Stay curious, keep learning, and be open to feedback. This adaptability will be key to sustaining your brand's presence on YouTube.

Above all, maintain your passion and enthusiasm for creating content. This energy will resonate with your audience and drive your channel's success. Thank you for choosing this guide as your companion in building a thriving YouTube presence for your brand. I wish you all the best in your creative endeavors.

ABOUT THE AUTHOR

Thomas J Elliott is an executive producer and creative director at global video production content agency Casual Films in Hong Kong who specializes in visual content storytelling.

He also dabbles in psychology and understanding human behaviour with a keen interest in what drives audiences to engage with visual stories and how to activate those audiences to make measurable actions that create rewarding interactions for brands, businesses, organizations, institutions and companies.

Here and throughout Asia, Australia, New Zealand and beyond, he has worked with an exciting list of international businesses, brands and agencies, including: 3HK, Aegis Media Dentsu, AIA, Alibaba, Autodesk, BBH, Buchanan Group, BUPA, Coca-Cola, Creativa, Disney, Genting Cruise Lines, Hasbro, Heinz, HSBC, IXL Appliances, KAO, Kraft, Maille, Manulife, Mattel, Microsoft, Nintendo, PZ Cussons, Prudential PLC, Reckitt Benckiser, Red Bull, Rolls-Royce, Shangri-La Hotels, STW Group, Subway, Unilever and many more...

He is a master cinematographer and the author of six books on visual content, film making and creative thinking.

He has won over 100+ prestigious international awards throughout his career and he is highly sought after as a creative, storyteller, strategist, director, cinematographer, educator, panellist, speaker and consultant.

Originally from Australia, Thomas lives in Hong Kong and Shenzhen with his family.

MORE BOOKS BY THOMAS JAMES ELLIOTT

Video Content Marketing: Mastering the art and science of creating great video content that delivers ROI!

What makes a video unforgettable? Thomas J Elliott, Executive Producer and Creative Director at Casual Films, breaks it down. He shows how leading brands, businesses, and organizations create videos that don't just look good—they deliver results.

This isn't about flashy effects or trends. It's about strategy. How do you connect with your audience? How do you turn views into value? Elliott shares practical insights, proven methods, and real-world examples.

Whether you're a marketer, a business owner, or a creative, this book gives you the tools to make videos that work. Because great content isn't just art—it's science.

And it pays off.

MORE BOOKS BY THOMAS JAMES ELLIOTT

Managing Creative Video People: And how not to go crazy doing it

Managing creative video teams can feel like trying to herd cats. Thomas J. Elliott, Executive Producer and Creative Director at Casual Films, knows this struggle firsthand. In *Managing Creative Video People and How Not to Go Crazy Doing It*, he shares hard-earned insights on leading passionate, unpredictable talent without losing your sanity.

This isn't just another management guide. It's a practical playbook for fostering creativity while keeping projects on track. Learn how to inspire, motivate, and collaborate with your team—without micromanaging.

The result? Better work, happier teams, and fewer headaches. If you've ever felt like creativity and deadlines don't mix, this book is your lifeline.

MORE BOOKS BY THOMAS JAMES ELLIOTT

PSYCHOLOGY IN VIDEO STORYTELLING: HOW TO CREATE BETTER VIDEO CONTENT MARKETING BY TAPPING INTO HOW YOUR AUDIENCE THINKS AND FEELS

What makes a video unforgettable? It's not just flashy visuals or clever editing. It's psychology.

In *Psychology in Video Storytelling*, Thomas James Elliott, an internationally recognised award-winning visual content creator, reveals how understanding your audience's emotions and thought processes can transform your videos. By applying psychological principles, you can craft stories that resonate deeply, drive action, and deliver real results.

This isn't about guesswork. It's about strategy. Learn how to connect with viewers on a human level, turning passive watchers into engaged advocates.

Want to create videos that truly matter? Start here.

MORE BOOKS BY THOMAS JAMES ELLIOTT

AI and Video Content Creation: The current state and future possibilities of AI in creating video content for your business

Video content is no longer just an option—it's a necessity. But how do you keep up in a world where technology evolves faster than ever before? Thomas J. Elliott, Executive Producer and Creative Director at Casual Films in Hong Kong and a globally recognised expert in video, breaks it down, in this must read new book.

AI is reshaping how businesses create videos. From automating edits to generating scripts, the possibilities are endless.

But where is this all heading? Thomas offers a clear, no-nonsense look at the tools transforming the industry today—and what's coming next and how it will impact not just how we watch videos but how we create them.

This isn't just about tech. It's about staying ahead. Whether you're a marketer, creator, or business owner, this book gives you the insights to adapt, innovate, and thrive. The future of video is here. Are you ready?

MORE BOOKS BY THOMAS JAMES ELLIOTT

Japanese Folk Horror Cinema: From Onibaba to Ringu and beyond

Step into the shadowy realm of Japanese Folk Horror with Thomas James Elliott, the acclaimed writer and filmmaker whose keen insights have captivated audiences worldwide. In "Japanese Folk Horror Cinema," Elliott embarks on an exhilarating journey through the haunting landscapes of this evocative genre, unveiling the deeply rooted fears, myths, and cultural narratives that have shaped its evolution.

From the sinister whispers of ancient spirits in "Onibaba" to the chilling allure of "Ringu," this meticulously crafted exploration traces the origins of folk horror and its grip on the Japanese psyche. With every page, readers are drawn into a world where folklore dances with the supernatural, and ancestral terrors lurk just beyond the veil of reality.

Elliott masterfully intertwines historical context, cinematic analysis, and personal reflection, inviting readers to confront their own fears and the universal human experiences of loss, longing, and the uncanny. As he dissects iconic films and lesser-known gems, he reveals the profound emotional connections that tie us to the past and the lingering echoes of tradition in modern narratives.

Prepare to be enthralled by a tapestry of chilling tales that resonate across generations. Whether you are a cinephile, a lover of folklore, or simply curious about the darker facets of humanity, "Japanese Folk Horror Cinema" promises not only to terrify but to illuminate, prompting profound questions about the nature of fear, memory, and the human experience.

Uncover the chilling depths of a genre that speaks to our deepest anxieties, and embark on a spellbinding journey through time, space, and the dark recesses of the soul. Discover Japan's most haunting stories, and let their spectral echoes linger long after the final page is turned.

MORE BOOKS BY THOMAS JAMES ELLIOTT

Giallo: From Bava to Argento and Beyond: A short history of Italian Murder Mystery Cinema

Step into the shadowy, stylish world of Giallo cinema. From Mario Bava's groundbreaking visuals to Dario Argento's haunting masterpieces, this book takes you on a journey through the genre's twisted tales of murder, mystery, and obsession.

Thomas James Elliott, a leading international voice in film and video, breaks down the key elements that define Giallo. The vivid colors. The chilling scores. The razor-sharp tension.

Why does this genre still captivate audiences? What makes it so unique?

If you've ever been drawn to the dark allure of Italian thrillers, this is your guide. A must-read for film lovers and mystery fans alike.

MORE BOOKS BY THOMAS JAMES ELLIOTT

The History of the American Slasher Film: From Peeping Tom and Psycho through to Halloween, Friday The 13th, Scream and beyond

From the dimly lit corridors of disturbing creativity to the silver screen's most iconic killers, "The History of the American Slasher Film" embarks on a comprehensive journey through the evolution of a genre that has both captivated and horrified audiences for decades.

Renowned filmmaker and author Thomas James Elliott explores the narratives that have shaped societal fears, the cultural milestones that ignited the slasher craze, and the enduring impact these films have left on our collective psyche.

Delving into the origins of the slasher phenomenon, Elliott illuminates the artistic choices and groundbreaking innovations that transformed simple horror tales into complex reflections of societal anxieties. Each chapter unravels the intricate interplay between a nation's history and its cinematic nightmares, inviting readers to confront their own emotions as they journey through fright and fascination.

With a blend of insightful analysis, personal anecdotes, and a rich tapestry of film history, this book offers a thrilling exploration that is as much about the films as it is about the viewers who dare to watch. Whether you are a die-hard fan or a curious novice, prepare yourself for a gripping exploration of fear, identity, and the sheer thrill of storytelling in "The History of the American Slasher Film."